THE HOME DECLUTTERING DIET

Organize Your Way to a Clean and Lean House

JENNIFER LIFFORD

founder of Clean & Scentsible

PAGE STREET
PUBLISHING CO.

PAGE STREET
PUBLISHING CO.

First published in 2017 by

Page Street Publishing Co.

27 Congress Street, Suite 105

Salem, MA 01970

www.pagestreetpublishing.com

Distributed by Macmillan, sales in Canada by The Canadian Manda Group.

20   19   18   17   1   2   3   4

ISBN-13: 978-1-62414-326-7

ISBN-10: 1-62414-326-1

Library of Congress Control Number: 2016954184

Cover and book design by Page Street Publishing Co.

Photography by Jennifer Lifford

Printed and bound in the United States

Page Street is proud to be a member of 1% for the Planet. Members donate one percent of their sales to one or more of the over 1,500 environmental and sustainability charities across the globe who participate in this program.

This book is dedicated to my amazing family
for all of their love, support and seemingly
endless messes that gave me lots of
material to work with.

TABLE OF CONTENTS

INTRODUCTION

A number of years ago, I decided that it was time to get serious about organizing our home. We had tons of "stuff," but could never seem to find what we needed. I always seemed to be organizing our spaces, but a few weeks later it was right back to the cluttered chaos. And then there were those areas of our home that were just too overwhelming to even begin to start organizing. I was spending so much time and energy trying to find things and was constantly frustrated with all of our junk that seemed to be everywhere. Although the house didn't look too bad on the surface, every drawer, closet and storage space was packed to the brim and completely dysfunctional. I could never really relax in our home because I always had a voice in my head nagging me to get things in order.

I knew that I needed to do something, but I wasn't quite sure where to start. The more I thought about what I needed to do to organize my home, the more I was reminded of the principles that we follow when we go on a typical diet to lose weight. By applying these strategies to organizing our home, I eventually developed The Home Decluttering Diet and was able to finally get our home organized once and for all.

The Home Decluttering Diet is a simple-to-follow organization plan that can be used to declutter and organize your entire home and provide you with the techniques and strategies to keep it that way for good. It's designed to take away those feelings of being overwhelmed and replace them with a solid plan to get started and continue moving forward. Each one of us is unique, and our vision of what our organized home is may be different, but this plan can help you achieve your goals whatever they may be.

Having an organized home is not about creating magazine-perfect rooms or adopting a completely minimalist lifestyle. It's about creating a calmer and more peaceful home where you can spend less time cleaning and doing things around the house and more time with your family doing the things you truly love. A home is meant to be lived in and well-loved, and it will get messy at times, but by eliminating those items that we don't need or use, and developing a solid organization plan for those items that we do love and have a purpose for, we can create a home that is both functional and cozy.

Jennifer Lifford

CHAPTER 1
GETTING STARTED ON THE HOME DECLUTTERING DIET

• •

Why I Chose The Home Decluttering Diet

Whenever I have difficulty trying to accomplish things, I try to relate back to something that I have more experience with and understand better. I struggled for years trying to get our home organized and, despite all of the time and energy I was putting into things, I was not really achieving any long-term success. I couldn't quite figure out what I was doing wrong.

After spending some time thinking about this, I started to reflect back on what I had learned in my university days and all of the physiology and sports medicine classes that I had taken. I definitely had many experiences with going on weight-loss diets and knew exactly what led to a successful (or unsuccessful) one. The more I thought about the basic diet principles associated with traditional weight loss, the more I thought about how this could be applied to losing all of the extra weight in our home.

It Takes a Long-Term Commitment

I think that it's safe to say that a disorganized house, like putting on weight, generally occurs over a longer period of time. We have kids, get pets, develop new hobbies and accumulate all of our clutter weight gradually over the years until one day it hits us that we are way too overloaded and drowning in all of our stuff. Sometimes we may not even recognize that the weight is creeping on as we become so accustomed to the chaos around us.

Unless you have the time to make getting organized a full-time job, it will likely take some time to go through everything and make your home the way that you would like it to be. And that's okay! When you go on a diet, you don't expect to lose it all in a month. Instead, you make a long-term commitment to gradually lose the weight over time through a series of lifestyle changes. Our homes will take time to lose the weight, too, so let go of the thought that you should be expected to do this all at once. It may not happen overnight, but it will happen!

• •

We Must Cut the Calories

Cutting back on the calories is one of the basic principles when going on a diet. Now imagine that every item that you bring into your home is food that you are feeding your home with. The items that you love and are useful can be thought of as healthy, lower-calorie food that is nourishing your home, while the items that are just sitting there in storage or clogging up your space are the empty calories that provide nothing of value. These objects might "taste" good for a short period, but over the long run they are just weighing you down and creating an unhealthy lifestyle. Even consuming too much of the healthy items can lead to weight gain if you don't control what you are letting in and sending back out. To maintain a healthy weight, the calories taken in must equal the calories that are put out. If we continuously allow calories into our homes, but don't get rid of some of the items that we already have, it's inevitable that our homes will eventually put the weight back on.

We Must Add in Some Healthy Exercises

Just as exercising is part of a healthy weight-loss diet, we must put in some work to help our homes lose (and eventually maintain) their weight. Organized storage systems need to be created to strengthen the structures of our homes and support the weight of all of the items that we accumulate. Remember that the more things you have, the more work you will need to do. If you want to do less, you need to have less. It's up to you to determine where this balance lies for you.

We Must Develop New Habits

In order to get our homes organized, and more importantly, to keep them that way, we need to identify our bad habits that created the chaos in the first place and learn new, healthier habits to replace them. Just as we have to develop new eating and exercise habits to lose weight, we need to develop new strategies and systems to create a clean and organized home. Eventually, these new habits become part of our typical day-to-day activities and become our regular routines, but it takes work and intentional planning to get there. If we don't change our old ways, it won't be long before the chaos returns.

Changing our habits and ways of thinking can often be a difficult process and it will likely take some hard work and time to do this. While some of us love change and can adapt quickly, others need to start small and build slowly on the new habits that they are forming. It may take some trial and error and a few tweaks here and there, but with a solid plan in place, we can replace those bad habits with healthier ones and lose the weight for good. The Home Decluttering Diet can really be done at any pace that you would like and can easily be tailored to whatever you want it to be.

Our Journeys Will All Be Different

Just like when it comes to losing weight, there is no one correct way to organize your home and no one strategy that will work for everyone. Some of you may only have a little weight to lose and just need to do some light decluttering and develop some new organization strategies to get yourself back on track. Others may have large amounts to lose and will need a longer period of time to accomplish their goals and learn new habits. Whatever your journey may look like, The Home Decluttering Diet can help guide you along your path, providing a basic backbone for you to build your own unique plan.

We Must Address What Got Us Here

Putting on weight doesn't always arise from simply eating too much food. Sometimes there are emotional or health struggles or significant changes in our lifestyles and stress levels that lead to the weight gain. Clutter, too, can result from many different situations and may present in many different forms. To truly get rid of the clutter from your life, it's important to understand how you got to this point so you can deal with any ongoing issues that are still of concern to you.

Clutter can arise from just being too busy or tired to deal with everything that is coming into your home or from not knowing proper systems and strategies to deal with it. It can result from serious health issues that you may have been going through or emotional events such as a death in the family or divorce. It can also be a result of poor money management and significant overspending. Whatever your reason (or reasons) may be, if you truly want to declutter and organize your home for good, these issues must be addressed. Don't be afraid to reach out to professionals if you feel that you may need additional help.

There is a Wide Range of Healthy

Just like a healthy body can come in many different shapes and sizes, so can our homes. Some of us prefer a more minimalist, uncluttered style while others like a little more meat on our bones. There's a wide range of what a healthy weight can look like, and it's up to you to determine what the ideal weight should look like for your home and your family. However, keep in mind that the more stuff you own, the bigger the space you will need and the more time you will need to commit to keeping things in order.

We Must Get Rid of the Excuses

One of the things that I am very good at is coming up with excuses, and I found that the excuses that I came up with for not organizing our home sounded exactly like the excuses I had for not starting a diet. "I just need to wait until after the holidays." "I just need to wait until I have more time." "I just need to wait until. . ."

Eventually, I came to the conclusion that I will likely never have any more time or energy than I have right now, and I need to make the best of what I do have. Whatever time and energy you have to work with—whether it's 15 minutes per day, a couple of hours per week or 5 hours per month—is better than doing nothing. Starting the journey is often the hardest part, so drop the excuses and simply begin.

We Must Think of the Rewards

We always need some kind of internal motivation or desire to drive us to do something new and challenging. The benefits always have to outweigh the costs. Like losing weight, I think many of us start out on these re-organization projects with so much gusto that we quickly burn ourselves out and give up. The bad quickly outweighs the good, and we shut down. The Home Decluttering Diet is designed to keep you going at a steady, manageable pace, so you can always keep the benefits of having more time to relax and spend time with your family, being more patient with your children and creating a calmer, more simplified life in the forefront of your mind. Think of what your own personal rewards will be and use them to keep you motivated. Continuously focus on what you have accomplished rather than what you still want to do.

In the end, getting organized is about clearing away all of that unwanted and unneeded weight so that you can truly enjoy those items that you do actually use and love. Having less stuff will give you more time to do other things. Have a clear vision of what you want the end result to be and think of this often as you move through this process.

How the Plan Works

The Home Decluttering Diet was originally designed as a yearlong plan to systematically target every area in my home, covering one room or space each month. I found that limiting my work to one room helped me to focus better on actually getting things done and made the process of organizing a whole house much less overwhelming. The order in which you target the rooms (with the exception of the 30-Day Home Detox [page 29], which should be done first) does not necessarily have to follow my plan, but I do feel that it's important to complete one room before moving on to the next.

You don't need to read through the entire book before beginning the plan, but I do recommended that you read Chapters 1 through 3 and Chapter 16 before starting. Refer back to these chapters frequently as you move through each room, as they will provide the basic tools that you need to declutter and organize any space that you come across. As you apply these techniques to each room, they should become easier every time you use them and will eventually just be integrated into your natural thought process.

A successful diet plan generally consists of three basic components: cutting back on calories and fueling your body with healthy food; exercising; and developing healthy lifestyle changes to keep the weight off. These same principles are applied with each room that we go through. The plan always starts with ways to cut your calories by aggressively decluttering your space and deciding which items you truly use and love and would like to keep. The second part of the program consists of organization exercises to help boost weight loss, and the final aspect focuses on tips, strategies and positive habits to help you maintain your home's healthy weight.

Once you have completed the first year of the plan and your home has shed most of the weight, I recommend that you continue to cycle back through the monthly plan as a maintenance program. With each year, this should require less and less work; however, it serves as a good reminder to stick with your healthy habits and allows you to re-assess and modify your organization plan over the years as your family grows and changes. Organizing your home is really an ongoing process with no specific end point, but if you follow the maintenance plan you will be able to keep up with the changes and continue to maintain a healthy, uncluttered home over the years.

Defining Your Personal Home Diet Goals

One of the things that I think is important to recognize with any diet plan is that we are all unique, and our end goals and vision of what healthy looks like may be very different. Before you even begin to start to get your home organized, take some time to think about what your own personal goals are and what you would like to accomplish throughout this process. Maybe you already have a vision of exactly what you want your home to be, but if not, here are some questions to ask yourself when developing your plan.

What Makes Me Happy in My Home?

We all want our homes to be filled with things that make us happy and every item and every space in your home should serve some purpose or bring you enjoyment. The whole idea behind getting organized is to allow you to enjoy these aspects of your life more while getting rid of those things that are just weighing you down and causing you stress and time. Think of favorite objects or furniture pieces that you want to be a focal point instead of being covered with clutter, or an organized hobby space where you can enjoy your craft instead of spending all of your time looking for things you need. Maybe what makes you happy is to just have a relaxing and clutter-free space to relax in or entertain your family and friends.

The level to which you need to organize and declutter to make you happy varies from person to person. Some people are happiest with a more minimalist lifestyle and are more relaxed when everything is tidy. They may have only a few special treasures displayed and choose to keep only the bare essentials. Others are happiest with their items more out in the open and don't actually view this as clutter. They like a more lived-in feel and are more tolerant of a little mess. In either case (or wherever you are in between), you must prioritize what you choose to keep in your home based on how much value and use they add to your life or how happy they make you.

What Things in My Home Cause Me Stress or Other Negative Emotions?

While we ideally want our home to be our happy place, an unorganized and dysfunctional home can often lead to stress and other negative emotions. Are you frequently frustrated because you can't find things? Do you have feelings of anxiety every time you have guests over to your home because it's so cluttered? Are you constantly late for appointments or getting the kids to school because it takes you so long to get ready in all of the chaos? Think about what you need to do to address these areas and how this can have a positive impact on your daily life.

We may also have objects in our homes that can cause a variety of negative emotions such as sadness, guilt or shame. For example, maybe you spent a lot of money on some new exercise equipment that you never ended up using. Every time you look at it, you are reminded about the money that you wasted on it and the fact that you still haven't managed to get in shape. You may have held on to that equipment for years, waiting for that day to come when you would suddenly be inspired to use it or magically have more time in your life. Let go of the object and let go of the guilt. It's not worth holding onto any item that's creating these negative emotions.

Do I Have Specific Places in My Home That are Particularly Weighing Me Down or Are There Certain Dysfunctional Systems that are Causing Me Particular Stress?

Take a few minutes to think about all of the areas in your home. Which spots are causing you and your family the most difficulty and add the most weight to your lives? For example, is it hard to make dinners or entertain because your kitchen is so cluttered? Can your kids not find their sports gear in the garage because it's so filled with items that have nowhere to go? Maybe your lack of paper organization has caused you to miss important payments and is leading to financial stress.

Recognizing what's not working in your home is an important step when it comes to designing your plan. Look at starting with these areas first in your diet plan, as organizing these spots will likely have the biggest impact on your day-to-day life and can help inspire you to continue on your organization journey.

CHAPTER 2

SHEDDING THE POUNDS: BASIC DECLUTTERING PRINCIPLES

One of the most important things that you must do on a diet is to cut your caloric intake, and decluttering your home is really about cutting all of those extra, empty calories. Just like you want to fill your body with nutrient-rich foods that will make you stronger and healthier, you want your home to be filled with items that you love and use.

Decluttering is the process of eliminating all of those excess items that are weighing you down from a space and time perspective as well as emotionally. It's about letting go of the past, enjoying the present and clearing the way for the future. Decluttering your home will not only make your space feel less cluttered, it will also help you to clear your mind. There will be less stuff to take care of, less running around trying to find things and more time to spend on what's really important to you.

Why You Need to Declutter

Every item in your home costs you something. It could be money, space, time or energy (or a combination of multiple factors), but there is always a cost associated with every item that you hold on to. If the item brings you happiness or is really useful in your life, the cost of keeping the item will likely be worth it. If, on the other hand, the item is not providing any current value, it's only preventing you from using that money, space, time and energy for things that are actually meaningful to you.

Clutter can also cause you to feel overwhelmed or anxious and may lead to a variety of other negative emotions such as guilt or depression. Similar to when someone puts on a lot of weight, we may not even realize that these emotions are starting to creep in until we suddenly feel so weighed down that we can hardly move. Getting rid of the clutter can help you get rid of these negative emotions and allow you to move on with other things in life that bring you more happiness. I think of this quote from Eleanor Brownn often when I'm decluttering: "Clutter is not just physical stuff. It's old ideas, toxic relationships and bad habits. Clutter is anything that does not support your better self." To be able to move forward, grow and embrace your current stage of life, you need to be able to let go of items from your past.

If your home is overweight and loaded down with clutter and you try to simply organize your stuff without going through an honest decluttering process, it's inevitable that the weight will return. It's like going on an extreme weight-loss diet for a few weeks and then returning to all of your old eating habits. The more stuff you keep, the more it will hold you back.

Eliminating clutter will get rid of those extra pounds that have been draining all of your energy and weighing you down. It will bring back peace to your home and allow you to truly enjoy the items that you do keep. While the process may be hard to start, the end result will be well worth the journey.

How to Declutter

I'm a big believer in the phrase, "The less stuff you own, the less that owns you." The more thorough you are with the decluttering process, the more successful your diet will be. There is absolutely no point wasting your time trying to organize items that are just weighing you down and are no longer useful. They will continue to cost you space and energy and provide nothing in return. Keeping these items around will not only cut down on your home weight loss but will also make it less likely that you will be able to keep the weight off that you did manage to get rid of. This was one of my biggest mistakes when I first began my organization process and the clutter just kept returning. Clutter just attracts more clutter.

No matter what size space or room you are working on, there is a basic decluttering process that should be followed. As you apply this to each new room, it will become easier and easier to follow until you eventually start to do it automatically.

Step 1: Prepare

Before you actually start to declutter, you need to have a plan in place and gather some basic supplies. You need garbage bags for all of the items that you are tossing in the trash as well as some bins or boxes to hold items that you will be donating or that belong elsewhere in your home. You also want to determine the amount of time that you have to work on your space, as this is going to have a big impact on what size project you will be able to declutter and organize. It's extremely important that you pick an area that you can actually finish within this time frame. For example, if you are working on decluttering your kitchen cabinets and only have an hour to spend on it, it may mean that you will just start with a cupboard or two and leave the other cabinets for another day. The last thing that you want to do is end up running out of time and creating a bigger mess than what you started with. If you are new to this process, I would recommend at least doubling the amount of time that you think a project will take—it's always better to have extra time left over at the end than to run out!

Step 2: Empty the Space

Once you have all of your supplies organized and are ready to get started, the first step in the decluttering process is to completely empty out the space that you are working on. In order to truly declutter and organize your space, you need to know what's actually there—and that means taking everything out! Once you have a fresh slate, it will be easier to determine what you want to keep and how you want to organize it. As you remove the items, sort them as you go into one of four categories: keep, toss, donate/sell or belongs elsewhere in your home.

KEEP—Only keep items that you actually use, need and/or truly love. Do not hold on to items that you wished you used or think that you might possibly need in the future. They will just weigh you down and prevent you from enjoying the things that you do love and need now.

TOSS—These items will be sent to the trash or recycling. This is for anything that is broken, missing parts or in very poor condition. If you think that you will have recycling items such as electronics, specific plastics or papers, it's best to use a second bag for this to keep it separate from the actual garbage. Ensure that you shred any paperwork with personal information on it before placing it into recycling. While I will often just refer to this category as "toss" as we go through the various rooms and spaces, please remember to use recycling for these unwanted items whenever possible.

DONATE/SELL—Donate/sell items are objects that are still in decent, working order that you no longer use or need. In future chapters I just refer to this category as "donate" but keep in mind that you can sell items in this category, too. You don't necessarily need to decide as you are decluttering if you will sell or donate the item, just make the decision that you will get rid of them in some manner. Refer to page 18 for some tips on deciding when to sell and when to donate. As an added note, unless you have specific items that you know your friends and family will love and use, it's best to just donate your items rather than give them to people you know so you're not unintentionally adding to their unused clutter.

BELONGS ELSEWHERE—One of the upsides when you are decluttering is that you will often find treasured items or other items that are useful to you that you had misplaced. As you are sorting through each area, place items that you still want but really belong elsewhere in your home into another pile. These items should be put away immediately in their proper places once you have finished the space you are working on. Don't try to put them away as you find them, as it will likely just lead to further distractions.

Step 3: Clean the Space

Having everything out of the space provides a great opportunity to give it a thorough cleaning. Depending on how cluttered it was, it may have been a while since you were able to get in there to really clean. Take a few minutes to give your space a good scrub down—wipe down shelves or drawers, dust into the corners, vacuum or sweep the flooring.

Step 4: Sort "Keep" Items into Categories

Sorting your items into categories helps you develop a good organization plan for storing your items and gives you a good idea of how much space each category requires. It also gives you a chance to identify duplicate items that you might not need or items that are outdated or missing parts (like electronic cords that you have no idea what they are for). Re-evaluate all of your "keep" items one more time as you are sorting through them to see if there is any extra weight that you can still get rid of.

Once you have completed all of these steps, you can then look at moving on to the next steps of actually organizing your items, developing effective storage solutions and putting your items back into their new home. These will all be discussed in the following chapter as well as in greater detail as we move through each of the room chapters.

Overcoming Your Decluttering Obstacles

While many people have the desire to get things decluttered and organized in their homes, it's not always such an easy thing to accomplish. Decluttering can often be a very time-consuming, overwhelming and emotionally draining experience, especially when you are first starting out. I will say, however, that once you overcome your initial obstacles, the process does get significantly easier. You start to see the benefits of letting your old items go and realize that you are not losing the memories just because you no longer have the items attached to them. I've given many items away that were extremely difficult to part with, but I can honestly say that I have never once regretted doing so.

Even when you understand the steps involved in decluttering, taking that first leap can be a scary experience and you may find that you are still holding back. Whatever the cause of your decluttering paralysis may be, you need to understand why you are having so much trouble before you can finally move past it. Take a few minutes to think about what is standing in the way of your goals and see if any of these common decluttering obstacles sound familiar to you.

Guilt

Our belongings should make us feel happy or in some way help us to improve our lives. So why are we holding on to all of those items that just make us feel guilty and weigh us down? I'm sure most of us have at least a few things that we have been holding on to out of pure guilt. Maybe you spent a lot of money on the item but never really used it, or it was a present from a favorite relative and you didn't want to hurt her feelings. No matter what the reason, keeping that item in the back of your closet will not help you to feel better. In fact, it will probably just make you feel worse. Get rid of it and get rid of that guilt! It may be hard to let go of, but you will feel so much lighter when you are done!

The Desire for Perfection and the Internet Effect

We are constantly bombarded by beautiful images of organized spaces with color coordinated and perfectly styled items. I'm sure we all have visions in our mind of what we ideally want our spaces to look like. We spend our time collecting ideas and waiting for that one day when we will have the time and the money to devote to creating that perfect space. Do not wait for that someday—get started now and do the best you can. Realize that organization is not the same as perfection. You can always add more or change things up in the future, so be proud of what you are able to accomplish today and let go of that often unattainable image of perfection.

The Item Represents Something That You Wish You Could Be

Do you have a whole closet filled with scrapbooking supplies that you have never even touched or a wonderful collection of sports equipment that has been sitting in your garage for years? Maybe in your mind you think that you should want to be that person that has a huge series of beautiful, completed scrapbooks or devotes hours each day to participating in various sports activities. Be honest with yourself and take some time to figure out what you really want to do with your spare time. Keeping things around that just remind you of what you are not doing will not help you achieve happiness. In fact, it will most likely have the reverse effect and just make you feel bad about yourself. It's your life and you need to do what makes you happy!

Emotional Attachment

I'm sure that this is a big one for almost everyone. Giving items away that we no longer use but we have some kind of personal attachment to can be hard. I must admit that I've even shed a few tears (and literally felt sick to my stomach) as I gave some of the kids' toys away, but I really have never had any regrets. It was just a brief moment of sadness as I let go of the past before being able to embrace the future. Remember that you are just letting go of the item; you are not letting go of the person or any of the memories attached to it. I'm not saying that you have to give every single item away—you can always keep a few favorite treasures from the past if you have the space. You just need to make sure that you contain it. Limit it to one box or tote and stick to it! If you are still having trouble letting go, try taking a photo of the item and writing your thoughts about it on the back of the photo or on a journaling card.

I Might Need It/Want It Someday

Chances are, if you haven't used an item in the past year, you will probably never use it again. In fact, once you have gotten rid of it, you will probably never even think of it again. And, on the off chance that you do need that kitchen gadget that has been sitting at the back of your kitchen cupboard for the past three years, you could always borrow one from someone else that actually uses one on a more regular basis. Live in the present and keep only what you currently need and use.

I Am Just Waiting Until . . .

This one is very similar to I Might Need It but can be even more negative. Your favorite jeans from when you were twenty that would fit perfectly if you could just lose those last few pounds. Or those roller skates that are sitting in the garage just until you suddenly have more time to use them. These items drag you down and remind you of what you don't have right now. Not only are they adding physical weight to your home, but they are also adding emotional weight to your mind. Get rid of them and don't hold onto somedays. And if you do happen to lose that weight, you really deserve to go on a little shopping spree anyways!

Lack of Time and Energy

Let's face it. We're all busy and have a finite amount of time and energy to spend each day. Starting your decluttering process is more about emotionally committing to the process rather than finding the time. Whether you choose to spend an hour once per week decluttering or do 15 to 20 minutes per day, it doesn't really matter. Any time that you devote to the process moves you one step closer to shedding some of those calories and getting things done. Set a realistic goal for what you can fit into your lifestyle and commit to it. Remember that getting things organized actually frees up more time in the long run because you will not be wasting time taking care of things that you do not use or looking for things that are buried in the clutter!

Whatever your hurdles may be, identifying and dealing with them is the only way that you can move past them. Think of how much lighter you will feel and how much more energy you will have when all of that extra weight is gone. Take a deep breath, visualize the end result and believe that you can overcome anything that's in your way.

To Sell or Not to Sell

If you have a lot of items that you are decluttering, selling at least some of them is an option that you can consider. Obviously, the big pro of selling is that you will make some money back from the items that you sell, but unfortunately, selling your items isn't always as simple as it sounds. Selling takes additional time and energy, and for those of us that have difficulties parting with our stuff, it can be one more excuse to not let it go. I honestly had boxes of stuff sitting in the basement for years waiting for me to get around to selling it. Not surprisingly, I never did get around to selling it and eventually ended up donating it.

Giving the items away to a charity or second-hand store is probably the easiest and quickest way to get items out of your home. If you have a lot of items, some charities will even come to your house to pick everything up and offer tax receipts that can provide a little financial benefit. For those of you who have a hard time letting go of things, this is probably your best bet to get rid of your stuff. All you need is just a few moments of courage and it will be gone! There's no time to change your mind or come up with excuses to keep things that you had originally intended to give away. While you don't get the same monetary return from this method, you know that the items will be going to good use and can take some pride in the fact that you are helping other families.

If you would like to explore some selling options, there are many different ways that you can do this, especially in today's society. Certain items tend to sell better with specific methods than others, and some options are more time consuming and labor intensive, so do your research to come up with the best option for you. I have listed some selling options below to help get you started, but there are many others that you could look into if this is the route you would like to go.

GARAGE SALES—Garage sales have been around for a long time and are still going strong in many areas during the warmer months. These usually work best if you have a large number of items to sell and, ideally, at least a few bigger-ticket items. Garage sale buyers tend to be huge bargain hunters, so if you don't like negotiating, this might not be the method for you. Personally, I find garage sales very hard emotionally as I have to say good-bye to each item one at a time, often for much, much, less than what I feel it's worth. If you are going to hold a garage sale, I strongly recommend that you don't bring your unsold items back into your home, but give them directly to a charity when the sale is completed. You may even be able to arrange to have everything picked up at a certain time at the end of the day.

FLEA MARKETS—These are basically large-scale garage sales with many different vendors. Obviously, the benefit is that it draws larger crowds and hopefully increases your chances of making a sale. The downside is that you have to pay upfront for a table or booth and spend extra time and energy taking all of your stuff over there and setting up. Look for specific flea markets that are tailored to what you are selling (for example, kids' items, antiques, etc.) and have your display set up nicely so it's visually appealing to buyers. Remember that you are also now competing for sales with many other vendors so you need to make yourself stand out.

CONSIGNMENT STORES—While they are not as popular as they used to be, consignment stores can still be an easy way to sell your items that are in new or gently used condition. Clothing and children's items tend to do best with this method, but you can also sell other items such as sports equipment or furniture. Many clothing stores will only look at items that are popular brand names and will sort through your items to see what they will actually accept, so make sure to pick your best items. Request that the consignment store does not return any unsold items; they will generally just donate them directly to charity if asked so you don't have to deal with them again.

LOCAL ONLINE SELLING SITES—While this can be a quick way of selling your items, you do usually have to price your items quite cheaply, especially if it's a common item that's frequently for sale. I do use these methods for bigger-ticket items but find that they are not worth my time if I am selling smaller things.

EBAY OR AMAZON—You can pretty much find any item imaginable on these two sites, so they can be good places to sell your stuff if you have a variety of different items, and they definitely target a huge audience of potential buyers. To get the most financial return, you ideally want to sell items that are in high demand that are not already saturated in the eBay listings. Some items can literally have millions of auctions running, so the chance of selling yours is not so high unless it really stands out in some way. Selling more expensive items or bundling your smaller items up into one auction will be more worth your while in terms of your time and financial gain. Remember that you have to pay a percentage of your sales in fees and you need to have knowledge of shipping methods and costs.

While the idea of getting money for your unused items does sound promising, selling your items isn't always the best way to go. It can really take a lot of time and effort to sell your items and you often get a much smaller rate of return than what you are hoping for. Even more importantly, it will extend the timeframe needed to actually get rid of your weight and get those items out of your home.

Before you decide whether or not to sell an item, take some time to think of the pros and cons of selling it and whether or not it will be worth it for you. If you are still unsure, answering the following questions will hopefully make your decision process a little bit easier.

Will the Item Be Worth My Time to Sell?
Remember that your time is not limitless and you want to use it wisely. Take into account how much money you will actually be making from your sale versus how much time will be involved. I always like to think of it in terms of an hourly rate. For example, if I am trying to sell the item for $5 and it will take approximately 30 minutes of my time in total (including taking photos, listing the item, emails with potential buyers), I will be working at a rate of $10 per hour. Set a minimum rate for yourself and stick to it!

Is the Item Going to Be In Demand?
There are so many forums for buying used items these days that it really is a buyers' market. If there are already a hundred items like yours listed, it's obviously going to be much harder to sell, and you are going to get a lesser rate for it. You also need to take into account the condition of the item and if it is still something that is relevant in today's market. VCRs just don't sell well these days.

Do I Have a Reasonable Expectation as to What I Will Make Off of the Item?
Sometimes it's hard to come up with a reasonable price for what you're selling, especially if you have an emotional attachment to it. Look at online selling sites to see what similar products are selling for. If you have collectibles, you can also check eBay to get a more realistic price point. Just remember to look at the items that have actually sold, as there are a ton of items on there that are priced higher but never sell. Your item is only worth something if someone actually wants to buy it!

Do I Actually Have the Time to Sell This?

If you are going to sell something, you need to be able to set a timeline for yourself and stick to it. If the item is not sold within that time, you need to just give it away. Be realistic—if you have a lot of things to get rid of, you won't have time to sell everything. Pick your best items to sell and donate the rest to lighten your load.

Can I Group Like Items Together into a Lot?

Selling similar items together in one lot will save you time and energy. You may have to take a little cut in the payment, but it's so much easier to unload all of the items at once.

In the end, the bottom line is this: the main goal of decluttering is to actually get rid of all of those items that you no longer need or use. If you can make some extra money on the side by selling some of your stuff, then that is great. If not, it's okay to just let your stuff go. The most important thing is that you are going to be getting it out of your home and losing those pounds! And that is a huge reward in itself.

Decluttering Tips

Pace Yourself

As you are going through this process, you need to remember that your house likely put on the extra weight over a long period of time, and, just like going on a diet, you can't expect to lose it all in a month or two. While it can always be exciting to get started on a new adventure, you don't want to get burned out before you have reached the finish line! If you lose the weight through a slow and steady process of decluttering and organizing and allow yourself to develop new, healthier habits over time, you'll be much more likely to keep the weight off in the end.

Be Aggressive with Your Decluttering

To do a thorough job of decluttering, you really need to be honest with yourself and learn to let things go. Evaluate every item and ask yourself if you use it, need it and/or love it. Does it add value to your life or is it just adding on the pounds? As hard as the decluttering process can be, think of all the perks that go with it such as creating a more peaceful and appealing environment, saving yourself time with cleaning and looking for things, and surrounding yourself with items that you love.

Sort the Remaining Items into "Stay" or "Go"

Once you have the items left that you want to keep, evaluate what items need to go back into the space and what items may be better stored elsewhere in your home. For those objects that you will be storing elsewhere, put them where they belong immediately after finishing your space, especially if they will be going in a room that you have already decluttered and organized. If you don't have anywhere for them to go in the new room, you need to evaluate if you really need to keep them or if there is another item you could get rid of to free up room.

Sleep on It

If you're really not sure if you should keep an item or not, set the item aside until the very end of your organization process and see if there is even space left for it. For me, seeing how nice my organized cupboards look is enough motivation to part with those so-so items that are left over.

Ask a Friend to Help

It can often be helpful to have an impartial (and honest!) friend around when you are going through the decluttering process. Since they don't have any emotional or financial attachment to your items, they can often provide some helpful input as to what you should keep and what you need to let go of.

Decluttering Questions to Ask Yourself

As you move through the decluttering process, there are a few simple questions that you can ask yourself if you are having difficulty deciding what you should keep and what you should let go. The more you intentionally think about these questions at the beginning of the process, the more they will just start to become ingrained into your natural thought process.

Do I Use This?

You shouldn't really have to think long about this. You either use the item or you don't. Take note that the question is not "Will I possibly use this one day?" As a rough rule of thumb, donate or sell non-seasonal items that have not been used in the past six months or seasonal items that were not used during the past season. For items that you use only once or twice per year, think if you could just borrow a similar one from a friend or family member rather than keep it around your own home.

Would I Buy This Today?

I find that this is a really helpful question especially when looking at decorative items or clothing. Ask yourself if you still love it and if it's still your style. Is it adding beauty or function to the space or is it just adding to the clutter? It's natural that your likes and styles will change over the years, so let those old items go that are no longer you.

Does This Help to Make My Life Easier?

There may be some items that you don't really need, but you do use regularly and they help to simplify things. You can definitely splurge on some items if they truly are useful to you!

Is This Item Extra?

How many wooden spoons do you really need? Do you really use all four cookie sheets? Evaluate what you need and use on a regular basis. Remember that you can always borrow items from friends or family for those one-time events. Choose your favorite and donate the extras!

Is This Item Functional?

If the item is not working or is missing pieces, toss it in the garbage. If it's something that you really want to keep or that would be of great value to someone else if it were repaired, keep it out and give yourself a deadline (such as by the end of the current month) for getting it fixed. Once the deadline has passed, toss the item if it's not yet functioning.

Can The Space That This Item Takes Up Be Reduced?

For items that I am keeping, I always look for ways to reduce their footprint. Can the packaging be removed for more condensed storage? Are there multiple bottles of the same product that can be combined? Can the item be transferred to a smaller container? Is there more appropriate storage that would make it easier to store and/or access? It's amazing what a little creativity can do!

CHAPTER 3

BUILDING STRENGTH: BASIC ORGANIZATION PRINCIPLES

• •

In addition to cutting calories, a successful diet plan always has a strong exercise component. In The Home Decluttering Diet, this exercise is in the form of developing organization solutions and long-term strategies that will help to improve the function of your space and strengthen your basic foundation. Think of it as building more muscle for your home. For each area of your home, I will give you a list of basic exercises to run through and show you a variety of projects and organization ideas that I have done in our home. Since each of our homes and organization goals are unique, they may not all work for you; however, they should serve as good building blocks for developing your own specific exercises.

An Organized House Versus a Tidy Home

While being organized definitely makes it much easier to keep a tidy home, having an organized house and having a tidy house don't necessarily go hand in hand. An organized home has a solid foundation in place to deal with all of the weight that it holds. Every item has a place and every item serves some purpose. We all know that our homes are going to get messy (especially if we have kids!) and an organized home is built to actually deal with these messes. If you have strong organization strategies in place and follow them regularly, cleaning up should actually be a fairly simple task.

A tidy house, on the other hand, has the outward appearance of looking organized but does not necessarily have the structures in place to handle the daily messes on a long-term basis. I used to have a tidy house. On most days, the counters looked fairly clutter-free and most of the items were picked up off the floor. The beds were usually made and the bathroom looked respectable. However, if you opened up a closet, you were likely to have something drop on your head. And if you pulled open the junk drawer the wrong way, it would fall off its tracks. It seemed like every space in the house was overflowing, and it was difficult to find things when I needed them.

In this case, when a mess happened, it would take me forever to get things back to a tidy state, and it caused a whole lot of stress in the process. I didn't know where to put things, and since I couldn't stand the clutter, I would just shove it into a random drawer or closet space. Since we have a fairly large house, I was able to use this technique for quite a while, but eventually the weight caught up with me and there was nowhere left to go. It was at this point that I knew that I either needed to get serious about getting organized or I would be left with a house that was constantly messy and chaotic.

• •

For those of you who feel like you are constantly dealing with an overwhelming mess that keeps returning, think about whether or not you have really been organizing or if you have just been tidying your home. Have you spent time actually getting rid of the clutter weight, or did you just hide the weight away temporarily? Have you really looked at creating effective storage and developing systems to keep your items organized, or are you just putting things away where you can to make your home look neat?

One of the most frequently asked questions that I get on my blog is, "Is your house always this tidy?" The short answer to this is no. Having an organized home doesn't mean that my house never gets messy. Life can get busy sometimes, and I might need to let go of some things around the house for a short period of time. However, now that I have a strong, solid organized base, I know that I will be able to get things back on track with just a little extra effort.

Basic Organization Strategies

Organizing your home can definitely be an overwhelming process if you don't have a solid plan in place, and it's often difficult to even know where to begin. No matter what space you are organizing or what level of chaos, there are some basic organization principles that can be applied to help guide you through almost any situation. The more you embrace these basic fundamentals, the quicker and easier it will be to get started (and to complete!) your projects.

Determine What Your Needs Are

Before you start any organization project, you want to take some time to reflect about what is currently working and not working in the space. Is there just too much stuff for the space? If so, you may need to cut more calories and be a little more aggressive with your decluttering. Is the space utilized to its maximum potential? Maybe you could add more vertical storage or configure your current system better. Are the items easily accessible and easy to put away? Determining exactly what the problems are in the space will help you get a clearer idea of what needs to be done and where you need to add some more muscle.

Organize By Zones

If you're organizing a room (or even a larger cupboard or closet), think about how you want the space to function and what kinds of activities you'll be doing there. Dividing a room into these smaller areas often makes the organization process less overwhelming and creates a very logical way to sort through your items. For example, in the kitchen you may have specific areas or cupboards dedicated to baking supplies, basic pantry staples or dishware. A linen closet may have a separate section for towels, linens, cleaning supplies or basic household staples such as toilet paper or paper towels. Take stock of all of the items that you want to return to the space and sort them into categories, keeping similar items together.

Keep Everything Accessible

The more often you use an item, the easier it should be to access. Store items that you use daily toward the front of your space and more toward eye level. Items used less frequently can be stored higher up or toward the back of your space. If you have deep cupboards, consider putting in a slider or pull-out bins to make items in the back more accessible or look for tiered shelving so items in the back are still visible. Remember to store items as close as possible to the area that you will be using them (especially for items that are used daily). Keep kid storage areas easy to reach with a designated spot for all of their supplies.

Optimize Your Space

Use your space to its full potential to get the maximum amount of storage and function. Add bars, hooks or small storage caddies to the inside of cupboard doors or along the narrow sidewalls in closets. For small storage areas, think vertically and add additional shelving higher up (for seasonal or less frequently used items) or add a wall storage unit. Don't be afraid to think outside the box to come up with multi-use pieces that will work for both storage and decoration.

Keep It Simple

Having a bunch of stacked boxes or other items may look pretty when you first organize everything, but it can be difficult to maintain. To get at something in the bottom box will require you to remove and put back other boxes. Ideally, you want to have every item accessible in just one step, meaning that you don't have to move two or three items out of the way to get to it. For items that you use less frequently, two-step storage can be used if needed. Remember that the easier something is to do, the more likely you (and your family!) will continue to follow through with it. The simpler the storage and the less time involved the better!

Choose Organization Products Wisely

I think of organization products like your workout clothes. If you purchase a bunch of clothes just because they are pretty without trying them on and making sure they fit, you're not going to use them and they will end up just creating more clutter. The same principle applies to the organization products that you choose. You want to make sure that you are buying items that will enhance and fit into the organization system that you have created instead of trying to come up with an organization system around the items that you purchase. For this reason, you want to look for bins, baskets or other organization products toward the end of the organization process. Make sure you take careful measurements of your space so you know exactly what will fit and work for you. I also like to look for items that I can return if it doesn't fit or function like I had envisioned.

Use Labels

Labels are particularly useful when you have multiple people using the same area—just because you know where an item goes, doesn't mean that the rest of your family will. Labels are also really helpful when you have storage in bins or boxes that are not transparent. If something is labeled, you know exactly where to go instead of pulling out random boxes to find what you are looking for. Chalkboard labels, vinyl lettering and other pretty labels can also add a decorative element to your space and are always a fun touch.

Do a Little Trial and Error

A truly organized space should be fairly easy to maintain, but it can sometimes take a little trial and error to get there. Once you have organized an area, give it a week or two and then do a quick check-in to see how things are going. If it's getting messy, look for reasons why. Is there still too much stuff? Does it take too many steps to put items back in their proper homes? Would any other organization items help? Address these needs and switch things up a little bit until you find what really works.

Re-Assess

Maintaining an organized home is really an ongoing process of re-evaluation and adaptation. As your family grows and changes, your organization needs will also likely change. By periodically reviewing all of the areas in your home, you can keep up with these changes and stay on top of things before they start to get out of control again. Busy areas of your house may need to be re-evaluated a couple of times per year whereas other areas may stay the same for years before needing to be switched up a bit.

Get the Whole Family Involved

Everyone that lives in your household should be contributing to how it functions at some level. The way that household tasks are divided can vary greatly from family to family, but everyone should have some responsibilities. Kids need to be taught and shown how to help out around the house (it doesn't just come automatically with age), so start working on this when they are young and add tasks slowly as they are capable. Even preschoolers can put their shoes in a bin, hang their coat up on a hook and clean up their own toys. It's much easier to create these basic organization habits in the first place than to have to go back and undo bad habits.

When you are organizing a new space, include the rest of the family in the plan. Including their input will likely help to increase their motivation and desire to participate in keeping things organized, and they may also have some great ideas to help organize the space that you didn't even think of. Make sure that everyone knows where things belong and explain clearly what's expected. This can sometimes take a bit of time, but be patient and consistent with following through with the plan.

CHAPTER 4

THE 30-DAY HOME DETOX

· ·

Now that you have a basic understanding of the decluttering and organizing principles, it's time to get going on the plan! Just as a detox diet helps to eliminate all of the toxins from your body, this 30-day home detox helps you clear out all of those items that are clogging up your home and adding to the unhealthy weight. The plan is designed to jump-start your decluttering and organization process and target those items that are obviously unloved and unused. While it may not get down to that deep clutter that we will address in each individual room, it will help to shed some quick pounds and drive your motivation and desire to keep going with the rest of The Home Decluttering Diet.

During the next 30 days, you'll be doing a quick rundown of your home and getting rid of as many items as you can in just 15 minutes per day. You can, of course, always do more; however, the idea is to keep it simple and easy to keep up with. We'll be going through each room more thoroughly in subsequent chapters, so this is not the time to be taking on any time-consuming projects or doing any major re-organizing. Just 15 minutes per day—anywhere you would like.

All you really need to get started with the detox are some garbage bags and some boxes or bins to put donation items in as well as items that belong elsewhere in your home. Keep these beside you with every space that you work on so you can sort all of your items as you go. You will likely be making multiple trips down to your local charity this month, so be prepared!

I have created a basic daily plan for the next 30 days to target pretty much every space in your home; however, I do realize that all of our spaces and needs are different. Feel free to just use this as a guideline and customize the plan to whatever will work for you. You can pick and choose whatever areas of your home need the most work. There are also some catch-up days built into the plan to allow for extra time in trouble spots or to work on areas that may be very specific to your needs. For extra-cluttered areas, you may want to spend 2 or 3 days going through things and skip some of the other tasks that are not really a problem for you. It's all up to you—it's your plan!

The 30-Day Home Detox Daily Plan

Day 1: Paperwork
Do you have a pile of paperwork (or two?) collecting on your kitchen counter or in your home office? Go through bills, receipts and any other paperwork, tossing (or shredding/recycling) what you don't need and sorting whatever is left over into its proper location. If you don't yet have a designated space for your paperwork to go, use a couple of file folders to hold important items that you need to keep—one folder for items that you need to do some kind of action with and one folder for items that just need to be filed. We will be going through the paperwork in much more detail when we tackle the home office, so don't get stressed if you don't have a solid organization plan in place.

Day 2: Front Entryway and Coat Closet/Mudroom
Donate any coats, shoes or accessories that you no longer use or need. If you are short on space, put items that are out of season into storage somewhere else in your home.

Day 3: Purse
Empty out all of the garbage and other items that you do not use regularly. Sort through receipts, filing what you need to keep and tossing the rest. Use a small pouch to hold makeup and other essentials so this can easily be transferred from purse to purse.

Day 4: Cleaning Supplies
Go through all of your cleaning supplies (wherever they may be!) and get rid of any products that you don't use. Use multipurpose cleaners to cut down on the amount of cleaning supplies needed or green cleaning products whenever possible. If you have multiple, partially filled bottles of the same product, combine them into one bottle. Toss any old cleaning rags or cloths that are at the end of their use. Commit to using old bottles up before opening up or purchasing new supplies.

Day 5: Fridge and Freezer
Remove all items from the fridge and freezer that have expired or that you know you will not use. Make note of items that are close to expiring and ensure that you use these items up first. Minimize packaging whenever possible to save space.

Day 6: Pantry and Other Dry Food Storage
Toss all items that are expired and get rid of anything that you know you will not use. Don't forget to go through all of those spices too and keep only what you use on a fairly regular basis. Place items that will be expiring soon or that you would like to use first toward the front of the cupboard.

Day 7: Free-for-All
This is your catch-up day if you didn't finish any of the above areas. If you are all caught up, pick the most cluttered area in your home and spend some time there.

Day 8: Kitchen Cabinets

Look for any obvious kitchen items that you do not use or have room for. Ensure that all food storage containers have matching lids and eliminate as many unnecessary kitchen gadgets, cookbooks and utensils as you can. If you're overwhelmed, just pick your messiest cabinet to address. Remember that during the detox you are just looking at those obvious items that you need to get rid of. We'll be doing a much more thorough organization of this space when we work on the kitchen.

Day 9: Medicine Cabinet/First Aid Supplies

Medicine is actually best stored outside of the bathroom in a cool, dry place out of the reach of children. Go through all medications and look for items that are expired or that you no longer need. Return expired medications to your local pharmacy for proper disposal.

Day 10: Dining Area

Commit to keeping your dining table clutter-free. Find storage solutions for all items that frequently find their way to the table such as crafts or kids' projects. Donate any dishes, serving ware or other items that you don't use regularly.

Day 11: Entertainment Area

Make sure all CDs or DVDs are in their proper cases and evaluate what you really use. Music and videos are so easily accessible through computers and mobile devices these days that CDs and DVDs may be a thing of the past.

Day 12: Magazines and Books

Let go of your magazine hoarding and get rid of any outdated editions. Cut out pages that you would like to keep and sort into a filing system or binder. Recycle or donate old books that you no longer read and sort the rest in a logical order.

Day 13: Junk Drawer

Get rid of everything that's not needed or used. Even though it's called a junk drawer, remember that it's for useful miscellaneous items, not random junk. If you have time, use inexpensive plastic containers to store similar items together. Put items that belong elsewhere away.

Day 14: Free-for-All

This is your catch-up day if you didn't finish any of the above areas. If you are all caught up, pick the most cluttered area in your home to go through.

Day 15: Desk

File away any needed paperwork and shred remaining papers with personal information. Sort smaller office supplies into handy containers and only keep products that you use. Get rid of any old calendars or planners.

Day 16: Bathroom Cabinets

Sort through your beauty products and keep only what you really use. Place items that are partially done toward the front of the cupboard so you can use those up first. Toss hotel shampoos or soaps if you have had them for a while and not used them.

Day 17: Linen Closet

Donate any linens that you no longer use that are still in good condition. Often, animal and homeless shelters are places that need linens most. Toss any items that are really dingy or have holes.

Day 18: Makeup

Toss anything that has expired, is cracked or is no longer your style. Pick your favorites and get rid of those other 10 lipstick tubes that you never wear. To find out more about the recommended shelf life for various makeup, go to page 74.

Day 19: Jewelry

Sort through all of your jewelry and decide what items you still wear. Toss costume jewelry pieces that are tarnished or broken and donate the rest. If you have more expensive jewelry items that are in need of repair or professional maintenance, keep these aside to take down to a jeweler as soon as you can.

Day 20: Bedroom Closet

Sort through your closet and donate items that you obviously don't wear or don't fit you. We will be going through the closet in much greater detail when we tackle the master bedroom (page 81), so just do what you can in your allotted time.

Day 21: Free-for-All

This is your catch-up day if you didn't finish any of the above areas. If you are all caught up, pick the most cluttered area in your home to go through.

Day 22: Sock and Underwear Drawer

Go through all of those socks and lingerie items. Make sure you have matching socks with no holes and toss items that are extremely worn or that you no longer wear.

Day 23: Nightstand

Clear off the tabletop and sort through drawers, keeping only what you would need before bed or during the night.

Day 24: Kids' Toys

This is always a fun one. Sort through toys to see what your kids still use (and have your kids help out on this one if they are old enough). Check to see that toys have all parts and are in working order before donating or selling. Toss the rest!

Day 25: Kids' Closets

Check to see what clothes still fit and donate the old ones or sort them into a labeled storage bin if you are saving them for younger children.

Day 26: Craft Space

Be ruthless and really evaluate what items you still need and use. Schools will often take extra supplies that you are looking to get rid of.

Day 27: Laundry Room
Sort through cupboards for any laundry products that are old or not used. Toss any unpaired socks that are hanging around.

Day 28: Free-for-All
This is your catch-up day if you didn't finish any of the above areas. If you are all caught up, pick the most cluttered area in your home to go through.

Day 29: Basement
Chances are this is one of the biggest sources of clutter. Set a timer and get rid of as many items as possible. Use large storage totes to store seasonal items together.

Day 30: Garage
This one is also a big clutter offender. Again, set a timer and collect as many items as you can that you no longer use or need.

Day 31: Car
Grab two bags—one for garbage and one for anything that needs to go back in the house. Put everything away in its proper place that you bring back into the house.

Tips for a Successful Detox

There's really only one main goal throughout these 30 days: to eliminate as much of your excess home weight as possible. Look primarily at all of that surface clutter that's always staring you in the face or those areas of your home that are a constant frustration for you. I realize that it's sometimes hard to get started, but once you do, it can really be exciting to see some of that weight come off!

I've put together some tips to keep in mind as you work your way through the next 30 days. These will hopefully help you to stay on track and optimize your home weight loss. Refer back to them as needed if you find yourself getting stuck or feel that you are starting to lose some of your motivation. Always remember your end goals and think about how light your home and mind will feel when all of that extra weight is gone!

Pace Yourself
Remember that this is just a quick, surface decluttering. We have a lot of organization ahead of us; don't get burned out now! We'll be going through all of these areas again in much greater detail when we work on the individual rooms—this detox is to lighten the load a bit so you don't have as much stuff to sort through. It has likely taken you years to accumulate all of your stuff, so don't feel bad if it takes you some time to get rid of it. Slow and steady wins the race!

Stay Focused
If you have a lot of decluttering to do, it can be really easy to get overwhelmed and get off track. Just remember you only have to do 15 minutes per day, and it's only one small space. If you're feeling inspired you can always do more, but pull out only what you have time to sort through and put back. You don't want to end up with a bigger mess than what you started with.

Keep an Organization Notebook or Binder

I recommend that you keep a notebook or binder to use throughout these 30 days as well as for the remainder of The Home Decluttering Diet. As you go through your spaces, you will likely have organization or project ideas that come to mind and, unless you write them down, you may not remember them when you get back to that room again. Your notebook can also serve as a place to write down inspirational quotes or thoughts that you may have to help encourage you on your journey. It doesn't have to be anything fancy—any notebook will do. Just make sure that it's specifically dedicated to your organization journey and that you have a designated spot for it in your home.

Don't Let Perfection Get in the Way

Again, this is a quick decluttering with the main focus being on shedding those pounds! Spend all of your time getting rid of things rather than getting caught up in making things look pretty and organized. There will be plenty of time for this later when we are working on the individual rooms. Don't think about it too much and just get started!

Be Flexible

While the plan is set up as a daily plan, we all know that life can sometimes get in the way. If you fall off of the plan for a couple of days, don't let this be an excuse to stop! You can either extend the detox for a few days at the end or do a couple of areas per day until you are caught up again. If the daily plan really doesn't work for you, just dedicate a longer period of time to work on your areas a couple of times per week instead. It's all about finding what works best for you.

Use the Timer Method

If you find that you are constantly getting distracted when you are working on your decluttering tasks, put on the timer. Pick a set amount of time, set your timer and commit to not doing anything else during this time. If your phone is a distraction, put it away where you can't hear it. Work as fast as you can while the timer is on and make it a game to see how many items you can come up with to get rid of. It may sound strange, but this method works extremely well for me.

Get Your Family Involved

If you really want to get a jump on that home weight loss, have your partner or kids (if they are old enough) join in on the plan. If they, too, get rid of 10 items per day, the weight will really fall off and you can double or triple the amount of clutter that you get rid of. Have them focus on areas that are specific to their items, and you will have more time for other areas of the house.

Refer Back to the Basic Decluttering Tips and Tricks

If you are having trouble getting started or letting go of items, keep referring back to the decluttering principles in Chapter 2 (page 13). The more you read them and start to practice them, the easier they become!

CHAPTER 5

SLIMMING DOWN THE KITCHEN

The kitchen truly is the heart of the home. It's where your family comes together for meals, where the kids sit and do their homework, and where you often spend the majority of your time entertaining. A clutter-free kitchen is not only more welcoming and relaxing, it also saves you time with your cooking and cleaning tasks. Take a few moments before you begin this space to think about what your end goals are and how you can make it easier to prepare and enjoy your meals. No matter what size space you have, a little work, some creative planning and smart storage solutions can transform it into a warm and inviting gathering spot for you and your family to enjoy.

Shedding the Pounds

Because the kitchen tends to be one the busiest rooms in the house, it's also one of the prime areas for collecting clutter. From unused kitchen gadgets to excessive piles of paperwork on the counter, kitchen clutter can quickly accumulate and pack on the pounds.

Before you start to do a thorough organization of the kitchen, you need to get rid of a little weight. The following list gives you an idea of what to look for during your decluttering process. Remember that this list just serves as a starting point for your decluttering and what you decide to keep and toss will be unique to you. Stick with the basic principles of decluttering outlined in Chapter 2 (page 13) and be ruthless when it comes to getting rid of items that you no longer need or use.

COOKBOOKS—Donate cookbooks that you no longer use. If you only use one or two recipes in a book, consider writing them out and storing them in a recipe box or binder rather than keeping the whole book. If you keep recipe magazines, tear out the pages that you would like to make and store them in a binder.

WOODEN SPOONS OR OTHER COOKING UTENSILS—Toss or donate any duplicate items or those items that you don't use.

DISHTOWELS—Go through all of your dishtowels and discard those that are past their prime. Evaluate your remaining towels to see if you actually need and use them all. If not, donate them or use them for rags. Animal shelters are often happy to take larger dishtowels.

BAKEWARE—Look for extra, old or unused cookie sheets, pie pans or muffin tins.

CLEANING SUPPLIES—Take stock of your cleaning supplies and toss those that you no longer use. If you have multiple bottles with the same product, combine them. Place those bottles that are close to empty toward the front of your stash so you will use them up first.

MIXING BOWLS—Keep only those bowls that you actually use. Stick with one main set or brand as much as possible for easy stacking.

COUNTERTOPS—Nothing makes your kitchen look messier than a cluttered countertop, and the clutter makes counters much more difficult to wipe down and keep clean. Get rid of unneeded papers, small appliances that are not used on a regular basis (you could just store these away if you still use them periodically) and decorative accessories that you do not love.

OVEN MITTS/HOT PADS—Toss any items that have holes or are significantly worn. Assess what items are extra that you don't really need to hold on to.

SPICES—You likely have at least a few spices that you never use that are still lurking in your cupboards. Toss any spices that you don't use or have lost their flavor and just stock the basic spices that you cook with regularly. You can always buy a small amount of bulk spices if you need something for a particular recipe down the line. Don't feel like you necessarily need to fill up a whole spice rack if you only use four or five basic spices.

CASSEROLES—While casseroles can be a great kitchen staple, sometimes you can have too much of a good thing. If you purchased it in a set, you may find that you use certain sizes of the dishes and not others. Evaluate what you use and donate the rest.

PANTRY ITEMS—Toss anything that is opened that you won't be using or items that are expired. If you have other unexpired items stocked that you don't think you will use, donate them to a food bank.

FRIDGE AND FREEZER—Toss items that are expired or look freezer burned. Check bottles and containers for expiration dates—you may be surprised at what you find!

FOOD STORAGE CONTAINERS—Match up lids and bottoms and toss anything that does not have a mate. Recycle or donate any remaining items that you no longer need or use.

CUTLERY—One full set of cutlery (plus a more formal set if needed) should be plenty, but I do also keep a few random spoons and forks to send in the kids' lunches in case they don't return.

DISHWARE, GLASSWARE AND COFFEE MUGS—Take stock of what you really need. Recycle any chipped or broken glasses. If you have extra, mismatched pieces, let them go. If you are a coffee mug collector, keep your favorites to put on display and donate the rest.

KITCHEN GADGETS—Kitchen gadgets always sound so amazing, but are often seldom used. Donate any items that you no longer use or if the function can be done with another item that you already have. Don't save items for someday—keep only what you currently use.

SMALL KITCHEN APPLIANCES—If you don't use it (or the task can really be done by another appliance), donate or sell it. You will get a big bang for your buck by getting rid of these items as they are often huge space suckers!

MEDICINE/VITAMINS—If you don't already store your medicine here, the kitchen is a great spot for it as long as it's kept in a cooler spot away from the steam of the stove or other appliances. Be sure all medications are up-to-date, you know what everything is for and it is stored safely away from little hands.

JUNK DRAWER—I think most of us have a junk drawer with miscellaneous items—make sure you actually need what you keep! Look for old batteries, extra office supplies, candles, tools, phone chargers or extra cords that you no longer use that you can get rid of.

OTHER ITEMS—Return all items that you would like to keep but don't belong in the kitchen to wherever they belong. Put them away immediately.

Building Strength: The Kitchen Exercise Program

A well thought-out organization plan in the kitchen is essential when it comes to keeping things running smoothly and efficiently and can result in a substantial decrease in the amount of work time needed for kitchen tasks. While it may initially be overwhelming to know where to start, dividing your kitchen into functional zones is one of the best ways to create more flow and function within your kitchen and really helps to define your space. Generally speaking, most people have five main zones in addition to their main eating area: a cooking and baking zone, a food prep zone, a food zone, a storage zone and a cleaning zone. Other areas, such as a beverage bar or coffee station, can also be set up depending on your needs and space limits. If you have a dining room just off of your kitchen, this can be another storage zone that you could use for extra dishware (if it's actually needed) or serving dishes.

The basic principle of dividing the room into zones is to group all similar items together and closest to the area where you use them. This gives you quick access to your items as you need them and makes it much easier for everyone to know where to put them away. Once you have decided where the various zones will be located, you can then start planning out how you want to organize your items and what storage solutions you may need.

The following guide gives you an idea of what is typically located in each zone so you can have an idea of how much cupboard and drawer space you want to allot. There's often a little bit of overlap between categories, so choose whatever items make the most sense to you and your family. If it's more functional to store something elsewhere, go for it!

Cooking and Baking Zone

This zone includes pots and pans, basic cooking utensils, bake ware, potholders, spices and any other basic cooking or baking items. It should be located as close to the stove and microwave as possible with the most commonly used items being the most accessible.

Food Prep Zone

This area contains everything you need to prepare meals like cutting boards, knives, measuring cups and spoons, and mixing bowls. Small appliances such as a mixer or blender can also be included here.

Food Zone

Even if you don't have a dedicated pantry, you should have some cupboards set aside specifically for food storage. Store boxed dry goods together by category, canned goods together and pantry staples together. If you buy a lot of items in bulk and have a smaller kitchen space, consider storing these items elsewhere and just keeping what you will use in a month in your pantry area.

Storage Zone

This zone is for all of your dish and glassware, silverware and storage food containers. Keep this area fairly close to the sink and dishwasher for quick and easy clean up.

Cleaning Zone

Generally, most people use the cupboard space under the sink to hold their kitchen cleaning items, but depending on your space and the amount of products that you have, you may have an additional cleaning cupboard or drawers allotted for this as well. This zone includes any kitchen or household cleaners, garbage, items used for washing the dishes, sponges or dishcloths.

Now that you have an idea of how you want your kitchen laid out, it's time to get organizing. The following kitchen exercises will help you to get your kitchen weight under control and allow you to develop an efficient and organized system that works for you and your family.

Organize the Kitchen Cabinets and Drawers

Organizing the kitchen cabinets and drawers will likely be the biggest and most time consuming task for the kitchen; however, it's well worth your time and makes a huge difference in how your kitchen functions. When it comes to organizing the kitchen cabinets, you can either do a couple of cupboards at a time or pull everything out from all of them and start from scratch. The benefit of doing it all at once is that it allows you to completely change up how and where you are storing your items; however, the downside is that it can take a lot of time and can often be an overwhelming process. If you have a lot to declutter and organize I would highly recommend breaking this project down into the smaller zones and just working on one area at a time. Remember to complete what you have started before moving on to the next space.

The following steps should be done for the cupboards and drawers in each of the zones. For some areas, such as the pantry and the cupboards under the kitchen sink, I've also provided more specific details and organization ideas in the following sections. As with all of the organization projects outlined in this book, feel free to put your own spin on things and do what makes sense for you and your specific needs.

Step 1: Empty the Cupboards

As you empty out the items, sort them into toss, donate and keep categories. Refer back to the decluttering suggestions in the Shedding the Pounds section (page 38) if needed.

Step 2: Clean and Prepare the Cupboards and Drawers

Clean and wipe down the sides and bottoms of all of the cabinets and drawers and dry completely. If they are showing some wear or scuffing, consider lining them with a shelf liner. These can be purchased in most home goods stores or you can make your own liners (see DIY Drawer Liners on page 98 for instructions). Make sure that whatever liner you choose is durable and can be wiped down easily.

Step 3: Sort the Keep Items

Go through all of the items in the keep pile and decide if they belong in the current zone. If not, place them in a cupboard or drawer in the zone where they belong. For the items that are remaining, sort them into similar categories and store these like items together.

Step 4: Decide on Storage Solutions

There are many, many organizational products when it comes to kitchen storage, so you need to have a good idea of what your needs actually are before deciding what products would be best for you. Don't limit yourself to the kitchen section of home goods stores when looking for ideas, and think outside of the box when it comes to creating specific solutions to meet your unique needs. You can often find some great items to use in the bath or home office supply sections of home goods or organization stores that can easily be adapted to kitchen storage.

DRAWERS—I highly recommend some form of drawer organizers or drawer dividers (see DIY Drawer Dividers on page 101) to further define your drawer space and allow you to give each item (or category) its own location within the drawer. This makes it easier to find whatever you are looking for, creates a lot less visual clutter and makes putting things back in the right spot much simpler. You can also find a variety of drawer organizers to store more specific items such as knives or spices if you choose to store these items in your drawers rather than on the counters.

LOWER CABINETS—If you have deep, lower cupboards, pull-out drawers allow you to easily reach items in the back without having to remove all of the contents from the front. These can be quite expensive, however, and may need to be custom-made depending on your cabinet sizing. If this isn't an option, be sure to store those items that you use regularly at the front of your cabinets and reserve the back for less frequently used or seasonal items. You can also look for shallow, plastic bins that fit into your cupboard that you can slide in and out to replicate the idea of drawers, or use smaller pullout drawers for smaller items. Use metal file folders to keep kitchen bake ware organized and easy to access.

UPPER CABINETS—Place all of your frequently used items within easy reach and store less used items up higher. For the higher shelves, store similar items in baskets or bins so you can just pull the basket down to find what you are looking for rather than having to stand on your tiptoes and rummage around in your cabinet. Lazy Susans are another great way to store spices, seasonings and other smaller items. For items on the top shelf that are difficult to reach, look for pull-down wire shelving units. These can be pulled down to access your items and then slide back up into place when you are done. If you have quite a bit of distance between your cupboard shelves, resulting in wasted vertical space, use wire racks to create multilevel shelving. This works especially well for storing dishware.

CABINET DOORS—If you are short on kitchen storage space, don't forget about the inside of your cabinet doors. They can actually provide a lot of extra storage and function! Store oven mitts, measuring cups and spoons (see page 45), or cleaning tools by using adhesive hooks or over-the-door hooks, or use file folders to hold frequently used recipes. You can also add chalkboard vinyl to keep a running grocery list or add some cork board to tack up your most commonly used recipes.

Step 5: Finishing Touches

Replace and organize all of your items into your chosen drawers and cupboard spaces, grouping all similar items together. Label sections as needed to ensure that everything gets put back in its correct space.

DIY Measuring Tool Storage

I love using the inside of our cupboard doors for storage. By hanging all of our measuring cups and spoons on the inside of the cupboard beside our stove, we can easily access them as we need for baking and cooking and free up some much needed drawer space at the same time. Chalkboard vinyl can be found in large craft supply stores or ordered online. Use markers that are not water-based (such as Chalk Ink® Artista Pro chalk pens) so they will not easily rub off if they accidentally get a little water on them.

All-purpose cleaner

Tape measure

Chalkboard vinyl

Scissors and/or a craft blade

Cutting mat

Credit card or other thin plastic card

Small, clear removable adhesive hooks

Chalk pens

Step 1: Prepare the Cupboard

Completely wipe down the cupboard door with an all-purpose cleaner to remove any oils and grime. Dry completely.

Step 2: Cut the Vinyl

Measure the dimensions on the cupboard door where you will install the vinyl. Transfer measurements to the back of the vinyl and cut with scissors or a craft blade and ruler on a cutting mat.

Step 3: Apply the Vinyl

Starting in one corner, line the vinyl up carefully and remove a couple of inches of the backing. Smooth with the credit card as you go to remove any small bubbles. If large bubbles start to form, you may need to pull the vinyl back a bit and apply again. Slowly peel the backing away and smooth with the credit card until all of the vinyl has been applied.

Step 4: Apply the Hooks

When spacing out the hooks, make sure that they (and whatever will be hanging from them) will not hit into any shelving in your cupboard and prevent the cupboard door from closing. To get an even alignment, I find that it's usually easiest to start in the middle of the cupboard and work outward. Measure the distance in between hooks to ensure even placement. Follow the instructions on the packaging for applying the hooks.

Step 5: Write Your Design

Have fun coming up with a creative design or simply use the chalk pen to label your measuring cups and spoons. I already had a measurement convertor that I added to my display, but you could also write out frequently used conversions with your chalk pens.

DIY Food Container Storage

Food containers can be one of the hardest items to keep organized in the kitchen. If you are purchasing new items, stick with one main brand to get similar shapes and sizes that stack easily. Square or rectangular containers are easier to organize space-wise compared to round containers and work better for storing food items in the fridge as well. One of the biggest problems with storing food containers is keeping the lids and bases together, and this easy lid storage has been the best solution that I have found. I found this basket in the bath section of a large home goods store.

All-purpose cleaner

Basket that will attach to hooks

Level

Clear removable adhesive hooks

Step 1: Prepare the Cupboard

Completely wipe down the cupboard door with an all-purpose cleaner to remove any oils and grime. Dry completely.

Step 2: Choose Basket Location

When choosing the basket position, make sure it is not located where it will prevent the cupboard from closing. Also check to make sure it fits when all of the lids are added. Mark lightly on the cupboard where you need the hooks to go and use the level to ensure that these are level.

Step 3: Attach the Hooks

Remove the adhesive back on the hooks and place them on the cupboard where you have marked. Follow the package directions before hanging your basket, as you often need to let these sit for an hour.

Step 4: Put it All Together

Hang the basket on the hooks and add the lids.

If you have the space in your cabinets and don't want to use the cupboard door for storage, you could also store the lids in a separate basket within the cupboard. For those of you that have a lot of random, small containers that you use for snacks, packed lunches or kids' food, store all of these in a pull-out drawer unit to keep them all contained in one spot.

Organize Under the Kitchen Sink

While this area is technically just another kitchen cabinet, I've given it its own section as it's probably the most frequently used area in the kitchen. It's also likely one of the most awkward spaces in the kitchen to organize due to pipes, garbage disposals and odd layouts. Since this is such a busy area and can hold quite a large number of products, you need to take advantage of all the space that's available and choose your storage solutions wisely. This cupboard can often contain dangerous chemicals, so be sure to have safety locks in place if you have small children in your home.

Step 1: Empty the Cupboards
This lets you see everything that is actually in there and gives you a chance to give the walls and floor of the cupboard a good cleaning. If the floor of the cupboards is in rough shape or you just want a little extra protection, line it with a shelf liner that can easily be wiped down.

Step 2: Declutter
Go through everything that you have taken out of the cupboard and decide what you really need to keep. Get rid of old cleaning supplies that you don't use or need, as well as any expired products. Pick cleaning supplies that can serve multiple purposes instead of having a different cleaning item for everything in the kitchen.

Step 3: Condense
I like to remove packaging as much as possible to save space and make everything more uniform. Dishwasher and garbage disposal tablets are kept in airtight glass jars and the packaging on smaller items is removed before storing them away in a pull-out drawer. If you tend to buy cleaning items in bulk packages, consider storing only a month's worth under the sink and keep the remainder of the product where you have more space. Make sure all products removed from their original packaging are labeled clearly.

Step 4: Choose Storage Solutions
Once you have pared down what you want to keep and have condensed your items as much as possible, you can then start grouping similar items together to give you an idea of what you need for storage. If you have deeper cupboards, a pull-out drawer works great to be able to easily access items that are toward the back of the cupboard, because if you can't see things, you likely won't use them! Look for storage items with smaller compartments to help keep all of the little things organized, or stackable bins if you have the space. Keep cleaning supplies in a portable caddy so you can easily take them with you to other areas of the house if need be.

If you are still short on space, look at the inside of your cabinet doors. There is a wide range of storage products available such as storage totes, towel bars and hooks that you can attach to cabinet doors. Removable adhesive hooks are another option for hanging towels or small cleaning tools. If you already have towel bars, add S hooks or shower curtain hooks to hang cleaning gloves or small cloths. Grommet kits are available at home building stores and can be used to add a hole to items that don't already have a hole or tag to hang them by.

Step 5: Finishing Touches

Place all of your items back into the space, making sure that you can easily access everything. If you have to remove a bunch of items to reach something, it likely won't stay organized in the long-term, so do a little arranging until everything works. Anything that you have removed from the original packaging should be clearly labeled so everyone knows what it is.

Organize the Pantry

Whether you have a large walk-in pantry or just a couple of cupboards designated as such, having an organized pantry is an important aspect of setting up a functional kitchen space. An organized pantry not only looks pretty, it saves you time and money and can help to cut down on food waste. With a little effort and some creativity, you really can create a functional pantry system that works for *you*.

Step 1: Pick the Location

Ideally your pantry will be located as close to where you do your meal prep and cooking as possible, although depending on the space available in your kitchen you may have to use another location. We actually have two cupboards in the kitchen for our main pantry items—one is right by the stove and the other is on the other side of the kitchen.

Step 2: Declutter and Clean

Empty everything out of your pantry spaces and toss any expired food or items that you won't eat. If you have non-perishable items that still have a good shelf life but you don't think you'll use them, donate them to a food bank. Give your pantry or cupboard spaces a thorough cleaning, wiping down all the sides and shelving and drying thoroughly.

Step 3: Reduce the Packaging

Packaging can take up a lot of space and the wide variety of shapes and sizes can make it difficult to organize. Invest in a good set of airtight containers to store common dry goods. Food stays fresher longer since it's always well sealed, and if you use clear containers, it's easy to see when you need to stock up again. Take packaged items such as granola bars or fruit cups out of their boxes and store them in bins.

Step 4: Organize Food into Zones

Organize your food items into zones such as baking items, canned items, school lunch items or snacks. It makes it easier for everyone to find what they are looking for and can save you time when it comes to meal prep. Keep the most often used zones within easy reach and close to the area that you use them.

Step 5: Choose Storage Solutions

Storage containers and cupboard organizers can definitely help organize your space, but they can also be pricey. Make sure that you have a good idea of your space restrictions and organization needs before you shop. If you have heavier or bulkier items, place them toward the bottom of the pantry, keep items that are most regularly used in the middle at eye level, and store those less frequently used, lighter items on the top.

DRY GOODS—I like to store my dry goods such as pasta, rice and cereal in clear airtight containers. It's easier to organize when everything is in a similarly shaped container rather than random packaging and it's easy to see when items need to be restocked. If you have kids especially, look for containers that are easy to use (I like the OXO® pop tops) as some styles can be difficult to put the lids on correctly. These can sometimes require a little bit of an investment, so shop sales and look for them at home discount stores. If you don't want to use containers, try getting some baskets to hold similar groups of items all together such as all of the pastas or all of the grains.

CANNED ITEMS—Tiered storage units are good for storing canned items so you can see items in the back. Look for rolling canned food storage units or plastic bins if you tend to stock up on a lot of similar items. For those of you who have a solid pantry door, wire storage units can easily be added.

SNACK FOODS—Dollar stores often have inexpensive bins and baskets that you can use to store snack foods like granola bars or fruit snacks. I keep crackers and chips in airtight containers rather than their original packaging to prevent them from getting stale quickly.

Step 6: Label All Items Clearly

Labels not only look pretty, they also let everyone know where things belong. Chalkboard labels work well and can easily be changed up as needed, but you can also use vinyl, metal label plates, tags or a label maker.

Step 7: Bulk Storage Alternatives

If you don't have room for a large pantry directly in your kitchen, look outside of the kitchen for additional food storage. Stock only what you need for a month in the kitchen and look for alternative places that you can store bulk food items. This could be in the garage, basement or other closet or cupboard space that you have in your home.

Organize the Medicine Cabinet

When we are organizing our homes, we often come across awkward areas or odd cupboard spaces that we don't quite know what to do with. Instead of just giving up on these spots, use a little creativity and planning to maximize the potential of the space. The side corner cupboard in our kitchen is a good example of one of these spaces—it's such an awkward size for storage and its location makes it difficult to reach items. Using the plastic corner bins that are designed for showers, I was able to turn it into a functional medicine cabinet that we use on a daily basis. The little bins can easily be taken in and out to give us quick access to all of our medications and vitamins and all of the space has been utilized.

Step 1: Choose the Location

While the kitchen might not be the first place that comes to mind for a medicine cabinet, it's actually a very practical place to keep your medicine and vitamins. Most medications need to be stored in a dry, cool place that is away from moisture, so a bathroom setting (even in a medicine cabinet) is not ideal. The kitchen provides a more moderate temperature (just be sure to keep it away from the oven or other heat producing appliances) and gives you easy access to any food and water that needs to be taken with the medication. All medications need to be stored away from children and pets and should be kept in their original, tamper-proof container as much as possible.

Step 2: Empty Everything Out and Clean

Take all of the medications out of your storage cabinet and gather up any other medications that you may have in other locations of your home. Check through everything and discard any unused, expired or outdated medication. Do not put medications into the garbage or down the toilet unless you know that it's safe to do so. Many pharmacies will gladly recycle your old medications for you or you can check your local municipal guidelines about safe disposal options. Over-the-counter medication can often be placed in a sealed bag with some kitty litter or coffee grounds for disposal, but again, it's best to check your local regulations first.

Step 3: Sort and Organize

If you have a limited amount of medications on hand, a single shelf or small bin may be enough to store everything in one place. If you have multiple members of your family taking different medications on a regular basis, you may wish to have a separate bin for each member in order to make things easier. Small baskets or bins also make it easier to access the medication, as you can quickly pull out the bin to find what you need rather than moving a bunch of bottles around in the cabinet. Label your bins clearly so you can easily identify what you have sorted.

Organize the Counters

Cluttered countertops not only make the whole kitchen look messy, they make it difficult to clean and wipe down the countertops properly. The number one rule for kitchen counters is that they should only be used for items that actually belong in the kitchen—mail, magazines and electronics need to find another home. Ideally, you want to reserve counter space for only those items that you use at least on a daily or maybe weekly basis. Contain the items that you do plan to leave on the counter to the back third of the counter space so that the rest of the space is free for kitchen prep and other work.

To make your counters look less visually cluttered, corral similar items on trays or in baskets to decrease the visual clutter and contain them in one area. This also helps with cleaning efficiency, as you can just remove one tray or basket to clean underneath instead of having to remove multiple items.

When you are choosing decorative accessories, look for items that not only suit your personality, but also add function to your space. For example, pretty fruit bowls, a vintage bread basket or glass bottles to hold dish and hand soap can all add charm to your kitchen while still providing a valuable function.

Organize the Fridge and Freezer

Creating and maintaining an organized fridge and freezer cuts down on food waste, saves you money on your grocery bill, makes food preparation quicker and allows you to come up with your grocery list a whole lot easier! The way you organize your fridge and freezer can vary greatly depending on the type of food items you frequently buy and the needs of your family. Remember that the main goal is to make everything as visible and as easily accessible as possible.

When working on the fridge and freezer, work as quickly as possible to minimize the amount of time your items are at room temperature. Pick either the fridge or freezer space to get started on and complete that first area before moving on to the other section. The steps that you should follow are the same for either space.

Step 1: Declutter and Clean
Remove all of the items from the fridge or freezer and wipe down the shelves. Remove and wash any bins or other removable parts in the sink with warm soapy water. Clean and wash the ice cube trays and storage in the freezer. Throw away all expired food or freezer-burned items as well as items that you know you will not eat before they expire.

Step 2: Sort the Items
Sort the food items out into similar categories such as produce, lunchmeat, cheese, bread or condiments. Assign specific areas of the fridge to each food category and label these sections if needed. In the freezer, you may have a section for frozen fruits and vegetables, meats or prepared meals.

Step 3: Decide on Storage Solutions
BINS AND CONTAINERS—Pull-out bins and other containers are an ideal way to organize similar food items together and make it much easier to find and access what you are looking for. I find that bins that run the full depth of the fridge work much better than smaller bins. It also prevents little items from getting stuck in the back of the fridge and forgotten. Each bin should be clearly labeled and limited to a specific food type. Clear containers are ideal so that you can easily find what you are looking for without having to open them up.

LAZY SUSAN—A rotating tray works very well in the fridge to allow access to items in the back of the fridge with just a spin of the tray. This works well for odd-sized jars or plastic containers such as yogurt or sour cream.

LEFTOVER STORAGE—When it comes to storage for leftover food, I prefer to use rectangular or square shaped bins as these take up less room if stored side by side and can easily be stacked since the shape is similar. Think of where you will store your leftovers in the fridge and choose containers to fit your space instead of trying to accommodate your fridge space to fit your containers.

SPECIALTY CONTAINERS—There are a variety of containers that are designed to specifically store certain items such as egg holders, soda can holders, onion containers, etc. While these can be helpful if you always have that particular item in the fridge, use them sparingly as they cannot be used for other functions and take up valuable space in your fridge.

ICE CUBE TRAYS—Look for covered ice cube trays to prevent water from spilling out of them when you load them into your freezer and to help keep your ice fresher for longer.

STACKABLE BINS—If you have a bottom freezer, look for stackable bins to store similar items and help keep your items organized. To get at items in the bottom of the freezer, you just lift up the top bin, instead of rummaging around looking for what you want. For smaller bins, stick with one main brand and shape so they fit together easily to maximize the space.

Step 4: Return the Food to the Fridge or Freezer and Reevaluate
Place all of your items back into the fridge or freezer keeping your zones in mind. Once everything is back in, evaluate how easy it is to reach and see everything. You can always play around with the food placement or shelf arrangement if things aren't working for you.

Organize the Junk Drawer

While I do think that most of us have a junk drawer in our homes, it should really be called a miscellaneous items drawer—but that's just not quite as catchy. A junk drawer is really just a spot for all of those random but useful items to be stored—batteries, flashlights and basic home maintenance. It should ideally be limited to one drawer in your home.

Step 1: Empty and Clean
It can be amazing what can come out of a junk drawer! Empty the drawer, sorting items as you go and tossing any garbage in the trash. Once it is empty, give the drawer a good cleaning.

Step 2: Organize by Zones

The junk drawer should not be a place that you throw all of those items that you just don't know what to do with—each item should have its own place where it belongs. Group similar items into categories such as home supplies, charging cords, batteries or whatever else you choose to store there.

Step 3: Divide and Conquer

To keep things organized in a junk drawer, you really need to divide up the space. Create some DIY Drawer Dividers (page 101) or use small bins or trays for each of your zones. Drawer organizers such as those used to store cutlery or home office supplies can also be used, just make sure that your items fit well into the pre-divided spaces so there is no wasted space. Label each section if needed and place your items back in the drawer.

Tips to Maintain a Healthy Kitchen Weight

- Do a quick maintenance check of your fridge and freezer each week when you are getting ready to write out your grocery list. Toss out any expired food items and put any items that are not in their proper location away. This is also a good time to give the shelves a wipe down as needed since the fridge will likely be a lot less full.

- Get in the habit of putting items away as you use them so your countertops do not become cluttered. It may take a little getting used to at first, but this will save you a lot of time and energy in the end. Remove all items from the counter at least once per month to give your counters a thorough cleaning under objects and into the corners.

- Once per year, empty out your cupboards to give them a good cleaning and reassess everything that you have stored in your cupboards to see if there's anything that you didn't use over the year. These items should be donated or tossed.

- Only buy what you need. If you are short on space, you might want to think twice about buying that tenth can of soup or another box of cereal. It can be tempting to load up when sales comes around, but you need to make sure that you are going to have the room to store it and that you are actually going to eat it before the expiration date hits. Even though you might have to pass up a few deals, having fewer food items on hand can actually save you money in the long run and will waste less food.

- Think twice about buying kitchen gadgets. Evaluate if the extra weight is really worth the cost of the space and money. If the item will be used on a regular basis and the function cannot be performed by any other item that you already have, the gadget may be worth it. If, on the other hand, you only use it a couple of times per year, it's probably better to just pass. When in doubt, don't purchase the item.

- When you buy new grocery items, place them toward the back of the cupboard or fridge so the old items can be used first. Make sure you don't open a new container until the old one is used and discarded. (This one seems to be a hard rule for my family to follow!)

- Medications should be checked on a regular basis to ensure that you have the basic supplies that you may need and that nothing has expired. Once you have everything organized, aim to do this once every three months or so.

CHAPTER 6

SCALING DOWN THE LIVING ROOM

• •

General Family Room Organization (page 60)

DIY Wooden Storage Crate (page 62)

Your family room should be a place where the whole family can hang out, relax and entertain. Since it generally serves as a multipurpose room, there can be challenges when organizing the wide variety of items that you want to include in the space. Organizing in terms of zones can make a huge difference in the flow of the room and provide a comfortable space for everyone to enjoy.

While some of you may have a separate living room and family room space, many of us just have one great room that is used for both family recreation and more formal entertaining. If you do have a separate living room, don't let the clutter spread through both rooms and do clearly define what should go in each space.

Shedding the Pounds

The family room area is often used as a dumping ground for all things, and a lot of the excess weight can actually be caused by items that don't even belong there. The more people that use the space, the more stuff tends to accumulate. If you feel that your family room is really cluttered, I recommend starting with all of the surface clutter (items that are just sitting out in plain sight) and getting any items out of the room that obviously don't belong there. Once this is done, you can then look at diving deeper into the clutter and evaluating which items you really need and which items have to go.

• •

BOOKS AND MAGAZINES—Keep only your favorite books and those that you will refer to again, and donate the rest. Recycle all out-of-date magazines. If there are specific articles that you would like to keep, cut out the pages and file them in a binder. Consider canceling any magazine subscriptions that you no longer love.

CDS—Keep only those CDs that you regularly listen to and love. If all of your music is now digital, transfer your favorite CDs to your computer. If you do have CDs that you would like to keep, store them in labeled storage boxes or toss out the case and just keep the CD in a CD binder to cut down on bulk.

DVDS—Keep only those DVDs that you still watch. Make sure all items that you are keeping are in their cases or stored in an alternative protective case.

GAMING DEVICES AND ACCESSORIES—You need your kids to help with this one! Go through all of the games and accessories and see which ones your children still use. Donate the rest of the items or trade them in at an electronic store for a store credit on future purchases. Toss any extra cords and make sure remaining cords are labeled.

TOYS AND KIDS' ITEMS—If you have any younger children, you probably have at least some toys in your family room. Keep toy storage contained to one area, a corner or far wall often works well, and only keep those toys that are actually played within this space.

MEDIA CENTER AND ACCESSORIES—Go through all of the items in your media center. Do all of the items work and do you still use them? If you no longer watch DVDs, get rid of the DVD player. Check all remotes and make sure that they are still needed. If you have a large collection of remotes, look into purchasing one remote that can be programmed for multiple devices.

PHOTOGRAPHS AND OTHER KEEPSAKES—While most recent photographs are likely digital, you may still have a large collection of loose photographs from the past. Sort through all of your photos and let go of photographs that are poor quality, that don't have particular meaning to you or your family or are duplicates. Organize all of your remaining photos in acid-free storage boxes.

DECORATIVE ITEMS—Take a look around at all of your decorative items. Do your favorite pieces stand out or are they lost in the clutter? Donate any items that you no longer love, do not have meaning to you or are no longer your style. If you have a large collection of collectible items, consider storing some away in storage and rotating your display. This will keep things fresh, still allow you to enjoy your collection and cut down on the clutter!

FAMILY GAMES—Toss any games that are missing important pieces. Sort through the remaining games and keep only those that your family still uses. Donate the rest. Store all games together in one location.

OTHER ITEMS—Return all items that you would like to keep but that don't belong in the family room to wherever they belong.

Building Strength: Exercises for Your Family Room and Living Room

The family room tends to be used for a variety of activities, so before you start organizing, you and your family should spend a little bit of time discussing what functional zones everyone would like to have included. Creating a solid organization system will allow everyone to enjoy the space and be able to work together to keep the weight off and the room organized.

I have listed some of the more common zones that are often included in a family room; however, you will likely not need them all and there are lots of different options that you can still come up with. Obviously the number of zones that you can set up will be at least partially dependent on the amount of space that you have available. Remember, it's your house, so create whatever suits your lifestyle and best meets the needs of your family.

ENTERTAINING ZONE—This area contains your sofas, coffee table and any surrounding chairs or end tables. It's where you may watch family movies together or visit with family and friends.

KIDS' ZONE—If you have younger children, you will likely need an area devoted to their items and specific activities. This area could include a small children's table with some art supplies, toy storage, comfy kids' chairs or board games.

MEDIA ZONE—The media zone holds all of your electronics—the television, cable box, speaker system, video game systems, etc.—in addition to all of the cords and accessories that tend to go with them. This area is often quick to collect clutter so it's an important area to focus on when organizing.

READING ZONE—Avid readers may wish to have a space specifically devoted to book storage or a quiet corner that they can curl up in and read a book.

CRAFT OR HOBBY ZONE—This zone would hold any supplies or equipment needed for your craft or hobby as well as a space for you to create. It could be something as simple as a portable rolling cart or basket to hold your supplies to a more sophisticated storage unit and desk space.

GAME ZONE—If your family loves to play games together, you may have a section devoted to game storage, or have a game table set up in a corner.

Remember that the basic ideas of using zones is to group all similar items together and closest to the area that you will be using them. This gives you quick access to your items and makes it much easier for everyone to know where to put them away. Once you've decided what zones you want in your family room (and living room if applicable) and where these zones should be located, you can then start planning out how you want to organize your items and what storage solutions you may need.

Here are the family room exercises that we will be working on in this chapter. While it looks like a very short list, the steps in the first exercise will need to be repeated with each zone so there's still quite a bit of work to do. I have provided a lot of different storage ideas, so choose whichever ones work best in your space. I encourage you to get your family involved with these exercises for any zones that they will be using.

General Family Room Organization

Now that you have an idea of what functions you would like your family room to serve, it's time to start implementing your organization system. Taking into account all of the zones that you would like to include, decide where each of these will roughly go in your room. Zones like the media zone may really only have one area where they will work due to the electrical outlets that they require and the large amount of space that's needed, so start with these zones first. Smaller, more flexible zones can then be added in where space allows.

The following steps should be followed for each zone that you would like to include in your family room or living room spaces:

Step 1: Empty Space and Clean

Empty everything out of the zone that you are working on and give the area a thorough cleaning. Get into corners, wipe down any drawers and clean along the baseboards. If you haven't washed the blinds and curtains for a while, now might be a good time to do so.

As you are emptying out items from the space, sort them into the keep, donate, toss and belongs elsewhere piles. If you come across items that are another family member's and you are not sure what to do with them, place them aside and have your family member look at what they still use and what can go. Refer back to the Shedding the Pounds section (page 116) if you are having trouble letting go of the weight.

Step 2: Sort Keep Items

Look at your pile of keep items and sort them into similar categories. If something fits better in another zone, put it away in that location. Take one more look at your keep items to see if there is anything else that should really be added to the donate or toss pile.

Step 3: Choose Storage Solutions

Once you know what items you will be storing, you can take a better look at the organization products out there. There are many different options to choose from depending on what zones you have created, your personal style and the amount of stuff that you need to store. You want to make sure that whatever you choose is simple and easy for the whole family to use. The following storage ideas can be used for a variety of zones.

FURNITURE STORAGE—When possible, purchase furniture that has built-in storage. Look for coffee tables or end tables with drawers or other closed storage to hide items that you would like out of sight. Ottomans can provide a place to put your feet up while still providing some hidden storage for toys, magazines or blankets. If you have a lot of electronics, an entertainment center can really help to control all of the clutter and provide the space and closed storage areas needed to give everything a dedicated home.

DECORATIVE BASKETS AND BINS—Large baskets and bins can hold rolled-up throw blankets to cuddle up with or extra pillows for movie nights or a cat nap on the sofa. Add some casters to wooden crates (see the DIY Wooden Storage Crates on page 62) and use them as storage bins. They can be kept in a corner when not in use and then rolled out into the space for play.

Bins or baskets can be used to keep smaller groups of similar items together. For example, a basket in your entertainment center can be used to hold video game controllers or other video game accessories. Storage bins can be used for CD, DVD or video game storage. Keep the shape and size of your storage bins similar— three bins that are the same will look much tidier than three random bins of different shapes and sizes.

TRAYS—Trays work well on flat surfaces such as coffee tables, side tables, or shelving units to hold a group of items together and make them appear less cluttered. A tray on your coffee table, for example, might hold a couple of magazines, the remote for the television and a decorative element or two. If all of these items were spread out over the coffee table it would look very messy, but because it's all contained within the tray, it looks more like an intentional display.

CUBE STORAGE—Cube storage is always an easy way to store toys and other kids' items and can also be used to store away electronic accessories such as video game controllers, CDs or DVDs. It tends to work better in more informal spaces, however, so if you plan on using the space a lot for formal entertaining, you might wish to look at other storage ideas.

SHELVING—There are many shelving options that you can look at in your family room—from custom built-in units to wall mounted shelves or stand-alone pieces. If you're using open shelving for storage, add some decorative elements into the space. Store books both vertically and horizontally for visual interest. Contain smaller items in decorative bins or use unique display pieces to hold your items out of sight. Keep some empty space in your shelving displays so the eye has a place to rest instead of having every area filled with stuff.

STORAGE LADDER—A storage ladder is a great way to fill in some vertical space and can be used in the family room to hang blankets or quilts, magazines, photo frames and more. While you can purchase these in stores, the DIY Storage Ladder on page 73 is an easy and inexpensive option that can be completed in a couple of hours. It can also be customized to the exact height and width that you would like so you can really maximize your space.

CORD CLUTTER—Containing and concealing electrical cords as much as possible can really help to tidy up your media zone. Start by untangling any cords that are clustered together and label each cord so you know where it leads. If there's a lot of extra cord, use a cord tie to gather up all of the excess. For multiple cords that are hanging down from DVD players, cable boxes, speakers or other electronics, try using a cable zipper to enclose all of the cables in one tube, While you still see the tube, it cuts down on the visual clutter.

Step 4: Add the Finishing Touches

Once you have added your storage, put all of the items away that you are keeping. Make sure that every item has its own designated spot. If there is extra space, add some personal touches to your family room such as a photo collage or gallery wall, some decorative throw pillows or a favorite memento from a family vacation.

DIY Wooden Storage Crate

If you need to add some extra storage to your family room, these crates add a rustic, farmhouse touch and provide a ton of extra storage. They can be customized to any size that you need and work great for holding larger toys, scrapbooks and photo albums, extra blankets, throw pillows and more.

All of the measurements listed below are based on a 30 x 17$\frac{1}{2}$-inch (76 x 45-cm) box using pine boards that were 5 inches wide and $\frac{5}{8}$ inches thick (13 x 1.6 cm). The steps can be easily adapted to build any size box that you would like and I have provided some guidance for this as well.

. . . .

24 feet (732 cm) of 5 inch (13 cm) pine tongue and groove boards

Circular saw or table saw

One 2 x 2 x 5-foot (61 x 61 x 152-cm) pine board

Sander

Wood glue

$\frac{1}{2}$-inch (13-mm) A/C plywood

Finishing nails

Screws

Framer's square

Paint and primer or wood stain (I used a walnut wood stain)

Casters

8 metal corner braces (optional)

Oil-rubbed bronze spray paint (optional)

Drawer pull

Step 1: Cut the Pieces to Size

Cut six pieces of tongue and groove board to 30-inches (76-cm). Cut six pieces of tongue and groove board to 16 inches (42 cm). Using a circular saw or table saw, cut the tongues off two longer pieces and two shorter pieces to make the top pieces for the box sides smooth. Cut the plywood to 28$\frac{3}{4}$ x 16$\frac{1}{4}$ (73 x 42 cm). Cut the 2 x 2s (61 x 61 cm) to 14$\frac{1}{4}$ inches (36 cm). Sand all rough edges.

Step 2: Attach the 2 x 2 Boards to the Side Panel of the Box

a. Fit the tongue and groove boards together for the front, back and sides of the box, making sure the tongueless boards are on the top edge. Glue the boards together using wood glue.

b. Starting with one of the sides of the box, line up the tongue and groove boards on the *outside* of the plywood sheet and place one of the 2 x 2 on top of the plywood sheet (it should be about flush with the top of the box but you can always sand it down a bit if it is slightly over). NOTE: The picture on the next page shows how I lined up the pieces before screwing the 2 x 2 to the pine boards but it is NOT where I attached the sides to the plywood base.

c. To attach the 2 x 2s to the tongue and groove boards, I first added some finishing nails to hold it in place and then used one screw in the middle to secure it.

(continued)

. . . .

2a

2b

2c

Repeat this with the 2 x 2s on the other side of the side panel. I then flipped it over and added two more finishing nails from the front (one on the top board and one on the bottom board) to secure the pine boards to the 2 x 2s. Repeat this with the other side panel. You should now have two completed side panels.

Step 3: Attach the Front and Back Panels of the Box

To attach the front and back of the box, use a framer's square to line up the sides so they are completely flush along the bottom and attach the front of the box to the 2 x 2 using finishing nails (I used 2 nails for each pine board). Secure with a screw toward the top and bottom corners. Repeat on all corners of the box.

Step 4: Add the Base of the Box

Turn the box upside down and add the plywood base by using 4 screws in each corner to attach it to the 2 x 2 blocks.

Step 5: Sand and Stain or Paint

Sand down the entire box. You may wish to sand the corners and edges a little extra for a more worn and rustic look. If you are painting, one coat of primer is recommended over the bare wood before painting a couple of coats of paint. If you choose to stain, apply the stain with a brush or lint-free rag and wipe away any excess.

Step 6: Add the Caster Wheels

Turn the crate upside down and determine where you would like to attach the casters. Use screws to secure.

Step 7: Add the Finishing Touches

Once the box has completely dried you can add whatever details you would like. I painted the corner braces and screws using two coats of an oil-rubbed bronze spray paint. Once they were dry, I attached them to the crate in all of the corners using the drill. The drawer pull was already oil-rubbed bronze so I just needed to attach this with screws.

Tips to Maintain a Healthy Weight in the Family Room and Living Room

- Since your whole family uses this space, your whole family should help maintain it. Remind the kids to put their video games away when they are done and teach younger kids how to put away their toys. If you have designed a simple storage system, it should be easy to do; it will just take a little time to form some new habits.

- If this space still tends to accumulate a lot of clutter that doesn't belong there, use a bin or basket to place these items in throughout the week. At the end of every week, take a few minutes and have each family member collect and put away whatever is theirs.

- Sort through and recycle old magazines every three months or so.

- If you read a book that you don't enjoy, donate it immediately rather than putting it back on your bookshelf, or skip purchasing books altogether and use the library or an e-reader.

- Re-evaluate your storage needs a couple of times per year to see if everything is still working for you. If certain areas tend to still get cluttered, see if there is anything that you can switch up.

CHAPTER 7

SHAVING DOWN THE BATHROOM

· ·

The bathroom is likely the first place that you go in the morning when you wake up, so a clutter-free bathroom space can create a calming mood to start your day off right. Having an organized bathroom space helps you get through your morning routines faster and out the door on time!

For those of you who have multiple bathrooms, I recommend starting with your main bathroom, as this is likely where the majority of the clutter resides. Keep all of your family's personal items contained to one main bathroom (or two if you have an en suite and kids' bathroom) and pare down the items in your secondary bathrooms (such as a powder room) to just the basic necessities.

Shedding the Pounds

The bathroom can be a difficult room to organize depending on how much space you have. Often we tend to have a lot more stuff than we have room for, which results in a cluttered and dysfunctional bathroom space. I must admit that I'm a total beauty product junkie and am the first one to get suckered in by pretty packaging or heavenly scents. Remember that many beauty products only last for a year or two or less, so you will only be able to use up so much within that time. Choose wisely, trial products first if possible, keep only what you love and think twice before you buy!

Before you get started on your bathroom organization, you need to slim things down and eliminate all of those items that you do not need, love or use. Remember that the less you have, the more you will be able to enjoy and use the items that you do keep.

· ·

TOWELS—Take a good look at your towels and see if they are all in good shape. For those that have seen better days, you can either use them for rags (if you actually need them!) or look at donating them to an animal shelter if they are still in decent condition. Determine how many towels you actually need to have. I limit ours to two bath towels per person plus a couple of extras for house guests and donate any extras.

COSMETICS—Start by going through all of your makeup and tossing those items that are past their expiration date (find more information on this on page 74). Next, go through what's remaining and determine what you actually wear and what you don't. Unfortunately, some colors just look better in the packaging than they do when we put them on! Keep only what you use and what makes you feel pretty.

MAKEUP BRUSHES—Go through all of your makeup brushes and pick out what you regularly use. Toss out any old brushes that may be losing fibers. Many times you buy a makeup brush set and only really need 2 or 3 of the 10 brushes that are included. Wash any remaining brushes with some gentle baby shampoo and dry before putting away.

HAIR ACCESSORIES—Go through any hair ties, elastics, headbands, etc. and toss those that you no longer wear. Store the remaining items together.

SKIN AND HAIR CARE PRODUCTS—Be ruthless. If it does not work for you, you do not use it (even if you wished you used it!) or if you prefer another product that serves the same purpose, let it go. Smell all products and place a small amount in your hand to make sure that it has not gone bad. I find that older products tend to take on more of a chemical smell or the texture is off. Recycle the plastic containers.

NAIL PRODUCTS—Nail polish has a longer shelf life than a lot of other beauty items. If stored properly out of direct sunlight and in a cool, dark area, it should last for at least a few years. Look for changes in texture (clumpy nail polish is bad!) to determine if it needs to be tossed rather than how long you have had it. Of course, just because it has not gone bad doesn't mean you should keep it if you don't use it, so make sure you still like the color and actually have the time to apply it. Store other nail accessories such as clippers, nail polish remover, files, etc. in a makeup tote or small bin.

MEDICATION—Ideally, medication should not be stored in the bathroom due to the temperature fluctuations and steam caused from baths and showers. Go through all medications and gather all items that have expired or you no longer need or use. Toss in the garbage if safe to do so or return them to the pharmacy for safe disposal. Find an alternative place to safely store your medication if you have been keeping it in the bathroom (see page 51 for details).

BEAUTY APPLIANCES—Sort through all of your beauty appliances such as hair dryers, straighteners, curlers, foot baths, shavers, etc. and evaluate what you use and what you don't. There always seems to be something that we hold on to for that someday when we'll have the time to use it, but if you haven't pulled it out in the last six months, the chances are that you never will. If you're holding on to that foot bath that you use once per year, maybe it would be better to get rid of it and just head out for a pedicure instead!

HAIRBRUSHES/COMBS—There seems to be a different size and shape hair brush for everything these days. Toss what you don't use and clean what you are keeping.

DECOR ITEMS—Take stock of any decor items that you have in the bathroom such as artwork, storage bins and other accessories. Ask yourself if it's adding to the space or if it's just producing clutter. Keep those items that you love and donate or toss any items that are no longer your style. When choosing decor items, especially in smaller spaces, look for items that are both functional and pretty.

SHOWER CURTAINS—Plastic shower curtains can be washed in the washing machine using warm (not hot) water and hung to dry. Eventually though, they do pass their prime and it is time to toss them for a new one. If you have a cloth shower curtain, do you still love it? Give it a wash if you do or donate or toss if it's time to update it. A new shower curtain is a fun and inexpensive way to give your bathroom new life!

TRIAL-SIZE BOTTLES—If you have a ton of trial-size bottles, it's time to use it or lose it. While it's nice to have one set of travel-size bottles for when you do go away, this is all you need! If you really love the product, commit to using up all of those little bottles first so you can get rid of the extra clutter. Items that are still sealed can be donated to a shelter, but most will not accept any packaging that has been used or opened.

SHAVING/HAIR REMOVAL PRODUCTS—Toss old razors and other items that you don't use (maybe that home waxing kit?). Test any electric razors to ensure that they are working properly and discard any extra accessories that you don't use.

BATHROOM CLEANING SUPPLIES—Take stock of your cleaning supplies and toss those that you no longer use. If you have multiple bottles with the same product, combine them. Place those bottles that are close to empty towards the front of your stash so you will use them up first. Look for cleaning products that can be used for multiple uses and minimize chemical cleaners as much as possible.

COUNTER CLUTTER—Counter space is generally prime real estate in the bathroom. Store as many items away as possible (while still keeping them accessible) and only keep items out that you use all the time (such as hand soap or hand lotion). Keep decorative items to a minimum depending on your space and make sure that you truly love them.

PERFUMES/COLOGNE—If you store perfume in your bathroom, ensure that it's stored away from heat vents and away from the steam of the shower. It may be better stored in another area of your home like your bedroom. Depending on how you store it, most perfume has a shelf life of about three to five years. Check all bottles to make sure that it's still good and you still love it (on you!). Think of how many bottles of perfume you have compared to how often you apply it. If you have more than you can possibly use, donate it while it's still good and keep your top two or three favorites.

BATH TOYS—If you have younger kids, sort through your bath toys to see what they still use and what they have grown out of. For those toys that you would like to keep, check to make sure that there is no mold anywhere especially on or in any squirt toys. Discard worn toys.

TOOTHBRUSHES—Toss any old toothbrushes. If you receive toothbrushes from the dentist that you don't use, recycle these as cleaning tools. It's ideal to store your toothbrush vertically either standing up in a cup or container or in a specific toothbrush holder so the bristles don't touch anything and it can dry properly. If this isn't possible, you can also find sterilizing caps that can fit over the top of the toothbrush to keep the bristles covered. Keep your toothbrush in a closed storage area rather than out on the counter when possible.

FIRST AID SUPPLIES—Check through all of your medical supplies to see what you don't need as well as what might need restocking. Check anything that has an expiration date to make sure that it's still good. See page 77 for further details on how to put together a first aid kit.

OTHER ITEMS—Return all items that you would like to keep but don't belong in the bathroom to wherever they belong. Put them away immediately.

Building Strength: Exercises for the Bathroom

Now that you have shed some pounds in the bathroom, it's time to get going on the organization process. Small bathroom spaces can be a challenge, but look at maximizing all of your vertical space as much as possible and creating specific storage solutions to fit your needs. If you have multiple bathrooms, start with your most used bathrooms first and aim to keep your secondary bathrooms as clutter-free as possible.

Organize the Bathroom Cabinets and Drawers

You likely have a lot of items that you need to fit into your bathroom cabinets and drawers, so utilizing every bit of storage space and choosing smart storage solutions is essential. If you're really short on cabinets or drawers (or don't have any!) I will talk about some alternate storage solutions at the end of this section as well.

Step 1: Empty Everything Out and Clean

Take everything out of the cabinets and sort items into your keep, toss and donate categories. Take some time to give the insides of cupboards and drawers a good cleaning, and wipe dry. Line with a liner if they are worn or you just want a fun pop of color (see DIY Drawer Liners on page 98).

Step 2: Declutter

The bathroom is notorious for collecting random bottles and jars of beauty supplies, hair products, soaps and lotions. Having too much stuff just makes it difficult to find and use what you actually have. Really pare down to what you truly use and what works for you. Little bottles might seem harmless enough, but taken all together they can really add to the clutter and dysfunction of your bathroom. Refer back to the Shedding the Pounds section (page 67) if you still have too much stuff. Sort keep items into similar categories such as makeup, dental care, hair products and shower and bath products.

Step 3: Choose Storage Solutions

DRAWERS—Some form of drawer dividers or organizers are a must in your bathroom to keep all of your little items organized and in their own space. There are a variety of options for these on the market to purchase or you can DIY your own drawer dividers (see page 101). If your drawers are deep enough, look for stackable drawer organizers to double your storage space.

CABINETS—Under-sink cabinets can be awkward for storing items and there's often a large amount of vertical space that goes unused. You can purchase specific adjustable shelving that is designed to work around piping or find stacking bins that fit on either side of the pipes. Wire racks that are designed for kitchen dish storage and slide out drawer units can also be used to provide multi-level storage. Keep all similar items grouped together in plastic bins or zipped pouches.

CABINET DOORS—If you are short on space, don't forget about the inside of your cabinet doors as they can provide a lot of extra storage if used correctly. Look for storage units that can hold awkward items such as your hairdryer or curling iron. Adhesive hooks are another option to hang face towels or bathroom cleaning cloths so they are easily accessible.

Step 4: Add Additional Storage if Needed

If you have done your best to utilize the space in your cabinets and drawers to its full potential and have completely decluttered everything you don't use or need but are still short on space, it's time to start thinking about where else you may be able to add some additional storage.

WALL STORAGE—Take a look around your bathroom and see where you may be able to add some additional shelves, a medicine cabinet or other wall storage unit. The space above your toilet is often a good spot for this, or smaller corner shelves may be a better fit for a really small space. While you can purchase pre-made floating shelves or other shelving units, a DIY option allows you to customize the size to exactly what you would like. The DIY Wooden Ledges (page 131) could work well in the bathroom for smaller jars with some basic bathroom necessities, or try the DIY Industrial Shelves (page 129) if you require deeper shelves. If you are going to be storing a lot of smaller items, contain them in bins or other storage units that are all the same so the space doesn't look as visually cluttered.

DOOR ORGANIZERS—Organizers, hooks or shoe organizers that can be hung over the back of your bathroom door (or on the inside of a bathroom closet door or cabinet) can be used to hold a variety of products. Look for coated metal or plastic storage units if you are going to be storing any wet items.

BINS AND BASKETS—A large basket on the floor can serve as storage for rolled up bath towels, while a smaller bin or basket can be used for extra toilet paper rolls or to store frequently used bath items. Baskets can also be hung from a towel bar using some S hooks or mounted to the wall with screws. If you are using shelving for a lot of storage, use square bins or baskets to contain similar groups of items so the space doesn't look so cluttered and items are easier to bring down to the counter when needed.

HOOKS—If you have a lot of towels to hang, hooks are more space efficient than towel bars. They can also double in function to hang a bathrobe or clothing items when you are taking a shower. Have a separate hook for each family member and make family members responsible for hanging up their own towels.

SHOWER AND BATH STORAGE—Ideally you want to keep all of the products that you regularly use in the bath or shower as close to that location as possible. There are many storage units on the market designed to hang from showerheads or stick to the side of your shower wall. Keep only one of each product and use it up before opening another bottle of the same product. If you have space around the tub or a built-in seat area in your shower, you could also just choose a plastic tote to hold your items.

STORAGE LADDER—If you are tight on space, a storage ladder can be used for hanging towels or baskets for extra storage without taking up a lot of room. It also adds some visual interest to the room and is great for renters that are not able to add any permanent storage to the space. These are available to purchase in many stores, or you can create your own easy and inexpensive version (see page 73).

FREE-STANDING STORAGE UNITS—If you don't have any built-in storage, try a free-standing storage unit or cabinet. Look for tall, thin units that you can place in a corner if you are short on floor space or choose a rolling cart that could be tucked away and then pulled out when needed.

DIY Storage Ladder

While this storage ladder is used in our bathroom, ladders can be used in almost any room of the house for added vertical storage and visual interest. If you don't want to use baskets you can just hang blankets, magazines, photo frames or whatever else you would like directly from the rungs or from hooks. We used 8 rungs on our ladder and they are about 11 inches (28 cm) in length. The ladder sides are 1 x 3 boards (actual dimensions $3/4$ by $2^1/2$ inches [19 by 63 mm] and the rungs are 1 x 2 boards (actual dimensions $3/4$ by $1^1/2$ inches [19 by 25 mm]). Since the ceiling is about 8 feet (244 cm) we made a 7-foot (213-cm) ladder.

If you want to make a wider ladder you will need more 1 x 2 boards. Based on your space and what you would like to store, choose the height and width for the ladder. Decide on baskets before building your ladder so you can determine the length of the rungs and the space between the rungs. This will be especially important if you would like more baskets on your ladder to ensure that you have enough space.

· ·

Saw

Two 1 x 3 boards, 8 feet (244 cm) long

One 1 x 2 board, 8 feet (244 cm) long

Sander

Rungs

Cardboard (optional)

Wood glue

$1^1/4$ inch (3 cm) wood screws

Drill

Wood putty

Paint or stain

Wire baskets

Shower curtain hangers or S hooks

Step 1: Cut the Wood Pieces to Length

Cut the 1 x 3s to 7-feet (213-cm). Cut the 1 x 2s into 11-inch (28-cm) sections. Sand off the rough edges.

Step 2: Mark the Spacing for the Rungs

The rungs are about $8^1/2$ inches (22 cm) apart. Mark the locations for the rungs on the sides, or cut spacers from cardboard or scrap the lumber to make sure that you place your rungs evenly.

Step 3: Assemble the Ladder

For the strongest ladder, glue and screw the rungs to the sides. Make sure the long side of the rung is parallel to the side of the ladder. Apply a small amount of glue to each end of a rung and position it between the sides. Drill pilot holes and drive two screws into each rung through the sides of the ladder.

Step 4: Fill in Holes

Once the ladder is assembled, fill in the screw holes with wood putty. Allow to dry, and then sand smooth.

Step 5: Finishing Touches

Paint or stain the ladder and allow it to dry. Attach your baskets using the S hooks and fill with whatever storage needs you have. You can also add some mason jars to the baskets and fill with items like toothbrushes, makeup brushes, Q-tips, lotions, etc.

· ·

Organize Your Makeup

When it comes to makeup, we often just use a very small percentage of what we have and stick with our familiar favorites despite having a whole collection of different products and colors. By paring things down to what you actually use and organizing your remaining cosmetics more effectively, you'll likely find that you're able to use your items more and will be much quicker with your routine.

Step 1: Purge

Gather up your makeup and pick out all of the products that you use and love. Try on colors that you may not have used in a while to make sure you still like them and will wear them. Just because it looks good in the package, doesn't mean that you will like it on yourself! Toss everything that you don't wear. Also look at makeup brushes, eyelash curlers, etc. and keep only those items that you use.

Step 2: Check Expiration Dates

While makeup generally doesn't have an expiration date written on it, it definitely does have a finite shelf-life from when you open the packaging. Check all of the items that you would like to keep and ensure that they are still in good condition. The following timeframes can vary somewhat depending on your climate and how your store your makeup, but you can use this as a rough guide. Alterations in texture or scent of the product are also other indicators that it's time for the trash.

- Concealer: up to 12 months

- Powder: 2 years

- Foundation: 12 months for water-based; 18 months for oil-based

- Pencil Eye Liner: up to 3 years

- Lip Liner: up to 3 years

- Eye Shadow: up to 3 years

- Mascara: 4 to 6 months

- Lipstick: 2 to 3 years (or less in hot climates)

Step 3: Choose Makeup Storage

To prolong the life of your makeup, it should ideally be stored away from extreme temperature changes and humidity, which can often be a challenge in the bathroom. While some of us may have a vanity in the bedroom to store makeup, most of us are probably stuck with using the bathroom for our primary storage. Store your makeup as far away as possible from the shower and keep it in a closed storage space to protect it.

How you choose to store your cosmetics largely depends on what space you have available, how much makeup you actually have and how portable you need your makeup to be. While there are many drawer organization units available specifically for cosmetics, kitchen utensil organizers, spice racks or other small bins can also work well for storing your makeup in a drawer. I used some mix-and-match stackable acrylic trays for my makeup with a different tray for each type of product. To keep things easily accessible, I just stacked the long tray and kept the smaller trays as a single level. Creating your own DIY Drawer Dividers (see page 101) is another inexpensive option for drawer storage, and compartments can be customized to the exact shapes and sizes that you would like.

If drawer space is not an option, look at portable makeup totes, baskets or other organizers that could be stored in a cupboard or bathroom closet. These can be brought out to the mirror when you need to apply your makeup, but then can be stored out of sight when you are not using them. This also provides an option to store your makeup in the bedroom or hallway closet if your bathroom gets particularly steamy and you are worried about damaging your makeup.

Makeup brushes are best stored upright in a container or kept in a makeup brush storage case to protect the fibers. Fill a vase with stones to set your brushes in and place it on the counter or in a cupboard, or use adhesive pockets on the inside of your cupboard doors to really maximize storage space.

Organize the Counter Spaces

Ideally you want to store as little as possible on your bathroom counters. Not only does counter clutter make the bathroom look messy, but it can also make cleaning your counters very difficult. If you do need to keep items on your counters, store them on trays or in baskets to make them look less visually cluttered and to make removing them for cleaning easier.

Tiered trays are also a great option for adding vertical storage space to your counters rather than taking up valuable square footage. Use canning jars or cups to corral similar items together and group them according to function. Add a few decorative touches, and it can be a pretty addition to your bathroom while still providing a lot of functional storage.

If you still have a lot of counter clutter when you are done, look back to the additional storage options discussed in the previous section to see if there are other areas in your bathroom that you can add storage.

Organize the Bathroom Closet

While not everyone has a dedicated closet space in their bathroom, it's definitely an added bonus for the busier bathrooms and can provide a huge amount of extra storage if utilized to its full potential. It may also allow you to store additional items in your bathroom such as household cleaning supplies, paper towels or bulk bathroom items that can be divided up with your other bathrooms that have less storage options.

Step 1: Empty Out the Closet and Clean

Take everything out of the closet, sorting items into the keep, toss, donate and belongs elsewhere piles as you go. Once it is empty, give it a good cleaning, especially into the corners where you might not have cleaned for a while.

Step 2: Decide on Zones

If you're going to be using the closet for multiple functions, think of what you want to store there and divide the closet up into smaller zones so that each category has its own space. You could have a cleaning zone for bathroom cleaning products and supplies, a storage zone for bulk toilet paper, paper towels or other larger items, or a kids' zone for bath toys and children's bath products. Keeping your zones in mind, sort all of your keep items into the appropriate categories, taking one last look to see if there is anything further that you can eliminate.

Step 3: Choose Storage Solutions

Assuming that your closet already has shelving, the bathroom closet is generally fairly easy to organize once you have your zones defined.

TOWEL STORAGE—Large towels can simply be folded and stacked on the shelving, while smaller towels such as face cloths and hand towels are often easier to keep organized when rolled or stacked in baskets or bins. Beach towels can also be stored in here if you have the space or can be stored elsewhere in seasonal storage when they are not being used regularly. If you do store them in the closet, keep them in a separate bin or shelving space so they don't get mixed up with the regular bath towels.

CLEANING SUPPLIES—I always like to have my bathroom stocked with the basic supplies needed to clean it stored in an easily accessibly location. This makes it much easier to do quick clean-ups as they arise instead of constantly having to haul out the cleaning supplies from another area of the house. Cleaning products should be kept in a tote or caddy so they are easily portable and don't get lost in the back of the closet. Utilize the sides of the closet wall by using adhesive hooks to hang wet cleaning towels.

KIDS' ITEMS—Keep bath toys corralled in a plastic bin or mesh storage bag. While a bag could also be hung in the bath area on a hook, you may want to keep this space free if you share the bathroom with your children. If your children use their own bath products, keep these stored in a small plastic bin or tote that can easily be carried to and from the bath and shower.

STORAGE ITEMS—Larger storage items can simply be placed on the shelf; however, smaller items stay more organized and are easier to retrieve if they are stored in bins or baskets. If you do use the closet for some extra storage, be sure to define what items actually belong there (such as extra toilet paper or paper towels) and which items do not.

FIRST AID SUPPLIES—A first aid kit is a must and it should be checked regularly to ensure that it's stocked with the basic necessities. See below for details on how to put together a proper first aid kit.

EXTRA STORAGE—If you have a solid door on the closet (as opposed to bi-fold doors), the back of the door can also provide a lot of extra storage space. Hang a shoe organizer, over the door hooks or totes, or add a wire storage unit specifically designed to hang on doors. The sides of the closet can also be used for storage with adhesive hooks to hang cleaning supplies or other storage needs. Since both of our kids often go to the pool, we have a pool bag already made up with their swim goggles, bathing suits, shampoo and soap so they can just grab a towel and their bag on the run.

Organize the First Aid Supplies

A properly stocked first aid kit is important to have in your home to cover any emergencies that may arise. While it will hopefully not be used often, it does provide peace of mind and will ensure that your family has some basic medical supplies if a disaster or medical emergency ever does hit. If you don't want to take the time to put your own first aid kit together, you can purchase pre-made kits through the Red Cross or other agencies.

You may choose to keep all of your first aid supplies in your bathroom, or pick another location in your home to store a full kit and just keep some basic supplies in your bathroom for the minor cuts and bruises that tend to arise on a more regular basis. Ensure that all of your family members know where the first aid kit (or kits) is kept so they can help out in an emergency if needed. The following list is what is recommended through the Red Cross for a first aid kit for a family of four. Adjust the supplies as needed if you have a bigger or smaller family.

- 2 absorbent compress dressings (5 x 9 inches [13 x 23 cm])
- 25 adhesive bandages (assorted sizes)
- 1 adhesive cloth tape (10 yards [9 m] x 1 inch [2.5 cm])
- 5 antibiotic ointment packets
- 5 antiseptic wipe packets
- 2 packets of aspirin (81 mg each)
- 1 blanket (space blanket)
- 1 breathing barrier (with one-way valve)
- 1 instant cold compress
- 2 pairs of non-latex gloves

- 2 hydrocortisone ointment packets
- Scissors
- 1 rolled bandage (3-inches [8-cm] wide)
- 1 rolled bandage (4-inches [10-cm] wide)
- 5 sterile gauze pads (3 x 3 inches [8 x 8 cm])
- 5 sterile gauze pads (4 x 4 inches [10 x 10 cm])
- Oral thermometer (non-mercury/non-glass)
- 2 triangular bandages
- Tweezers
- Flashlight
- First aid instruction booklet

These items can be stored in a backpack or other portable carry case. If your storage case does not have separate storage areas to keep things organized, use plastic resealable bags to organize your supplies by category (i.e., all adhesive bandages together, all bandages and gauze pads together, all medications together, etc.). Check your first aid kit regularly to ensure that it is fully stocked, the batteries in the flashlight are working and no items have expired.

DIY Minor First Aid Kit

While our main first aid kit is stored with our emergency preparedness kit in the basement, I like to have some basic supplies on hand in our bathroom to deal more with the day-to-day issues that arise—scrapes, mosquito bites, slivers, etc. This kit is portable and makes it super easy for everyone to find what they're looking for at a glance.

Step 1: Find a Storage Container and Choose Your Storage Location
I like plastic craft totes with customizable dividers for this project as the individual slots make it easy to access all of the supplies and the dividers can be moved around to fit whatever supplies you stock. Alternatively, you can also use zippered travel bags or storage totes specifically designed for first aid supplies.

Step 2: Stock Your Items
For this smaller kit, think about what your family needs for medical supplies on a fairly regular basis. You can always access your main first aid kit if a bigger medical emergency occurs. Here's a list of what we have included in ours to serve as a starting point for you:

- Adhesive bandages in a variety of shapes and sizes
- Blister pads
- Alcohol wipes
- Styptic pencil (to stop bleeding)
- Tweezers

- Scissors
- Antiseptic hand gel
- Cool compresses
- Insect bite relief
- Antibiotic ointment

Step 3: Put It All Together
Group similar items together in the container. I used some scrapbook paper and stickers to decorate ours up but you can always just label it as first aid supplies. Check the kit every six months or so to see if additional items are needed or if any items have expired.

Tips to Maintain a Healthy Bathroom Weight

- Ask for trial beauty products when possible before investing in new items to ensure that you actually like them and will use them. If you do purchase an item and then realize that it's really not for you, don't hold on to it!

- If you bring home shampoos or soaps from hotels, use them right away. Don't let them add up! Commit to completely using one item up and getting rid of the packaging before opening up another container of the same product.

- Avoid stocking up too much on beauty supplies as your styles and preferences may change more frequently. Also keep in mind the shelf-life of the products you purchase to ensure that you are not buying more than you can actually use.

- Keep your bathroom counters as clutter-free as possible to make cleaning easier and faster.

- Hang up and use your bath towels for more than one use so you don't need to keep so many towels on hand.

- Consolidate your beauty products as much as possible such as using a 2-in-1 shampoo conditioner, or not using a separate eye cream from your regular face cream.

CHAPTER 8

WINDING DOWN THE MASTER BEDROOM

. . . .

The master bedroom is often a neglected space in our homes and can frequently be used as a dumping ground for clutter since it's not generally seen by guests. Ideally your bedroom should be a private retreat for you and your partner—a favorite spot where you can unwind, rest and have a little time to yourselves. By cutting down on the extra weight and organizing your remaining items, you can create a spot of your own that you truly love.

If you have a dedicated guest bedroom in your home, this is the time to work on that space as well. The steps and thought process will all be the same—you just won't have all of the clothing to worry about! Just as you want to create a bedroom retreat for yourself, the guest bedroom should also be a cozy and relaxing place for your guests to unwind when they need some quiet time on their own.

Shedding the Weight

If your bedroom has packed on the weight over the years, now is the time to remove it! With busy lifestyles, we can often put ourselves last and, as a result, you may not have spent much time dealing with the master bedroom. Piles of laundry, clothing items that you never wear, accessories and other items that don't even belong in the bedroom can be weighing you down and preventing you from having a healthy, happy space that you can relax in. Take some time this month to trim off the weight and create a peaceful place to recharge.

. . . .

CLOTHING—This is likely the biggest source of excessive weight in the master bedroom, so take some time to sort through your clothing items and toss or donate those items that you don't wear. If it's not something that you love and would purchase today, it's time for it to go, as you will likely never wear it again. Also evaluate your old standby clothes that you always seem to gravitate to. Are they still in good condition or are they starting to look overly worn? Toss any items that are past their prime.

SHOES—Get rid of any shoes that you no longer use or that you find uncomfortable.

PURSES AND BAGS—Purses and bags are items that we tend to collect but not always use. A pretty purse is not useful to you if it just sits in your closet, so choose your favorites and actually use them! Donate those purses that are extra or just collecting dust. Toss purses that are worn or dingy or have broken zippers and straps that are not worth getting fixed.

BELTS, SCARVES AND OTHER ACCESSORIES—Donate any items that no longer fit your body or your style. For those items that you still like, make sure that they actually match your outfits. If you don't have anything to wear them with and they've been hanging around for a while, let them go.

JEWELRY—Sort through all of your precious and costume jewelry. Set any items aside that you need to get repaired. Toss tarnished costume jewelry, earrings without a mate or broken items that are not worth being repaired. If you have more expensive jewelry that you no longer like, consider selling it or taking it to a jeweler to have a custom piece made using your stones and precious metal.

HATS—Try on all hats and keep only those that you wear and still like.

BEDDING—Toss any bedding that has holes or is overly worn. If some of the material is still in good shape, you may be able to donate it to an animal shelter or think of other useful ways that you could repurpose it. Donate any comforters, quilts or sheet sets that you no longer use. Two or three sheet sets as well as a summer and winter cover should be all that you need for each room. Look at all of your pillows and toss those that are old, heavily stained or have gone flat. Donate any extra pillows or decorative pillows that you no longer love.

BEDSIDE DRAWERS—Only keep items here that you use just before bed, need first thing in the morning or may need throughout the night. All other items should be stored elsewhere.

LINGERIE AND UNDERWEAR—Toss out all items that have holes or are overly worn. Check that all remaining items still fit, are something that you need and are something that flatters your body. If not, it's time for it to go!

SOCKS—Ensure that all of your socks have a matching pair and toss any with holes or those that have lost their elastic.

OTHER ITEMS—Return all items that you would like to keep, but don't belong in your bedroom, to wherever they belong.

Building Strength: Exercises for the Master Bedroom

The master bedroom should be a private retreat for just you and your partner, so take some time to create a spot that you will look forward to going to.

Organize the Master Closet

Decluttering all of those unworn and unloved clothes and accessories can be a little overwhelming, but it will be so much easier to dress your best if you only have a closet filled with items that you love and clothing that fits you well. Having an organized closet system allows you to see all of your items better and encourages you to put together some new outfit ideas and actually wear all of your clothes!

Step 1: Empty Everything Out and Clean

As I'm sure you've learned by now, you must start the organization process by taking everything out of the space. Sometimes it's quite amazing to see all of the weight that you were able to pack into a closet and perhaps the number of items that you never even knew you had or had forgotten about. As you take your items out, sort everything into keep, donate, toss and belongs elsewhere and unsure piles. Once your closet is empty, take some time to dust and wipe down shelves and storage bins and vacuum the floors and into corners that may not have been cleaned for a while.

Step 2: Purge

Sort all of the items in your keep pile into categories such as shirts, pants, shoes, bags and jewelery, and take a closer look at the items that you have chosen to keep. Now is the time to get rid of everything that you have not used in the past 12 months. If you don't wear it and feel good in it, it's time for it to go! I realize that, for most of us, this is much easier said than done, but you must be ruthless here!

Try on everything that you placed in your unsure pile and give yourself a good look in the mirror. Does the item fit you well and highlight your assets? Does it go with any other items in your closet or has it been sitting there because you have nothing to wear with it? Now is the time to really be honest. If this is hard for you, consider inviting over a good friend who doesn't mind speaking her mind.

Clothing is one of those items that people tend to hold onto in the hopes that they will someday be able to wear it. Often these items are too small and you are hoping they will eventually fit, but it could also be formal wear that you just never have the opportunity to wear or office attire that you no longer use now that you stay at home with your children. If there is a specific reason that you are not fitting into or using some of your clothing (such as a pregnancy or illness or if you are currently on a diet), try putting the items that do not fit into a storage bin and commit to getting rid of them after a predetermined amount of time if you are still not using them.

Add any items that you have decided not to keep to your donate or toss pile. When it comes to selling clothing and accessories, remember that unless your items are in high demand, vintage or designer, it's unlikely that you will be able to get a lot of money for them and it's probably not worth your time to sell them. Donating to charity is generally easiest, and your clothes can often make a big difference in other people's lives.

Step 3: Organize by Zones

Now that you've decluttered, it's time to put everything back into the closet. Before you start, think about how you would like things organized and what types of items you have to store. Your aim is to design a system that you can maintain easily on a daily basis, keeping items as visible and as accessible as possible. Those items that are not seen should be clearly labeled.

I like to organize the zones in my closet by item, keeping all jeans together, all tops together, all handbags together, etc. I also have some bins that serve a specific function. For example, all of my workout wear is in one bin, all of my sleepwear is in another bin, purses are in another, etc. Keep these labeled so that you know where everything belongs.

Keeping the design of your space in mind, decide which items you will hang, what items can be folded on shelves, and what items would work best in bins or baskets. Use matching hangers for those items that you are hanging. Wood or velvet-covered hangers work better than the metal hangers to maintain your clothing's shape. Place items that are used most often in the front and middle sections of your closet space if possible. If you have a small closet, consider storing out of season or rarely used items elsewhere or install a high shelf to hold bins for these items.

Step 4: Maximize the Space and Decide on Storage Solutions

To get the most function out of your closet, you need to use as much of the space as possible. Think of using all of the vertical storage space between the floor and the ceiling and store out-of-season or less-used items on higher shelves. Look at the sides of the closet or closet doors to see if any other storage options could be added. The following list gives you some additional storage possibilities that you may not currently be using.

BINS—The place between the floor and where your clothes hang is the perfect place to store some extra shoes or clear plastic bins on wheels for your accessories.

DOOR—If you have a solid door, add some hooks for hats or bags or use a pocket organizer to hold shoes or scarves.

ORGANIZERS—Use a hanging sweater organizer on your closet rod to hold heavy sweaters and other items that you prefer to fold rather than hang. You can use the different panels for different storage items—it's not just for sweaters.

DRESSERS—If you do not have double clothing rod hangers, move a dresser into the closet below your shorter hanging clothes for extra drawer space. For an inexpensive option, look for a second-hand dresser and refinish it or paint as needed.

CURTAINS—Remove the closet doors and hang curtains. This makes it easier to get into the far corners of the closet.

HOOKS—Add hooks to the walls or sides of storage units. If you don't want to do any drilling into the walls, use repositionable adhesive hooks. They come in a variety of strengths and sizes, can easily be switched around as your needs change, and work great for hanging necklaces, purses, bags or hats.

There is definitely not a shortage of closet organization products out there. You can find some great options almost anywhere. Just remember to figure out what items you need to store and the space that you have available first, before heading out to look for the products that you need. See page 86 for more specific ideas on organizing clothing and page 87 for more ideas on organizing your accessories.

Step 5: Add the Final Touches

Your closet will be one of the first things that you see in the morning and one of the last things that you see at night, so it might as well be pretty. Pick some of your favorite clothing or accessory items such as shoes, purses or colorful scarves and put them on display. Hang a favorite picture or inspirational quote on the wall, or place a favorite art piece on an empty shelving space. Line the back of the closet or your shelves with wallpaper or paint it a fun color. I always find that the prettier the space, the more motivated I am to keep it tidy and organized.

Organize Your Clothes

Keeping your clothes organized saves you time, allows you to easily put new outfits together and makes the task of getting dressed each morning so much more pleasant. Storing your clothes properly can also help them to maintain their shape and last longer, which can save you quite a bit of money in the long run. Assuming that you have already aggressively purged all of those clothing items that you no longer wear and love, this section focuses more on specific ways to organize your clothing.

HANGING ITEMS—While it's not necessarily the best space-saving method, hanging your clothing on hangers is perhaps the quickest and easiest way to store them and allows you to see all of your items in one glance. Skip the cheap, metal hangers and go for a matching set of velvet or wood hangers to keep a uniform look. These hangers not only look nicer, but also help to keep the shape of your clothes better and prevent them from falling off. Maximize your hanging space by having a rod on both the top and bottom of your closet where possible and just keep a smaller section for full hanging items such as long coats and dresses.

The simplest way to organize your hanging clothes is by type, grouping all of your jeans together, all of your pants together, all of your shirts together, etc. If you wish, you can go one step further and organize these categories by color.

Another option is to group your clothing by function such as keeping all of your work clothes together, all of your casual wear together, etc.

OPEN SHELF STORAGE—Open shelf storage takes a little more effort to maintain, but is often the best space-saving option for items that need to be folded. When using this method, use shelf dividers to keep all of your items neatly stacked. Keep your stacks limited to 4 or 5 items if possible so that it's not a huge hassle to get items out of the middle or bottom of the stack. If you need to fold items but don't want to use your shelving space, purchase a hanging sweater organizer to hang from a clothing rod.

BINS—Storing clothing in bins is a great space-saving method and helps to keep all of your similar items contained to one space. Bins can easily be pulled on and off the shelves for quick access to your clothing and help to decrease the visual clutter of open storage. If you do store your items using this method, be sure to file your clothing items like file folders rather than stack them on top of each other so you can look into the bin and see all of the items at the same time. Fold all of your items to approximately the same size and shape to make it easier to keep them organized.

DRAWERS—If you are tight on space, drawers can be a very space-efficient method for storing clothing. If you do opt to store T-shirts, jeans and other clothing items in your drawers, use the vertical file storage method as described in the bin section to ensure that you can always see what's in there and that no items get lost in the bottom.

While I personally prefer to hang my clothes whenever I can, I do like to use drawers to store items that I don't necessarily want to display such as socks or lingerie. Socks and underwear can easily be kept organized with small drawer dividers or stored in smaller baskets within the drawer itself to keep them separated into categories. If you really like to be organized, fold socks (rather than balling them up) to put less strain on the elastic and roll longer stockings up. For a lower-maintenance method of storing your socks and underwear, you can just use small bins in your closet to separate your socks, underwear and other undergarments and just toss them in the appropriate bin instead of folding.

Organize Your Accessories

Accessories are a fun way to add personal style to your outfits, but if they are hard to find you will likely forget (or not have the time!) to use them. Again, the main goal when organizing your accessories is to make them more visible and accessible so that you can actually use what you have.

FOOTWEAR—Store frequently used footwear on shelves or on the floor space under your lower clothing rods. Tall boots can be hung on clips from a clothing rod or stored on a shoe rack or the floor using boot shapers or other objects (such as pool noodles or a rolled-up magazine) to keep them standing up. Hanging shoe dividers can be hung in the closet or from the back of your closet door to store a large number of shoes. A narrow shoe cabinet can fully use vertical space.

PURSES AND BAGS—If you have the space, display a couple of your favorite purses on a shelf for a decorative touch. Frequently used purses can be hung on hooks for easy access or stored in a labeled bin that's easy to access. Out-of-season purses should be stored on higher shelves or placed in seasonal storage if you do not have the space in your closet to accommodate them during the off-season.

SCARVES—Scarves can be hung on closet rods with a scarf organizer or rolled up and stored in a labeled box. Try to store them in one layer so you can see everything in the box at one glance, or keep in-season scarves on the top layer and have a bottom layer for scarves that are out of season. If you just have a couple of scarves, they could also be hung from hooks.

BELTS—Belts can be hung from hooks, clothing hangers or a specific belt organizer, or you can roll them up and store them in a labeled bin or drawer.

JEWELRY—There are many different jewelry organization systems on the market from jewelry boxes and acrylic drawer organizers to wall-mounted displays and jewelry trees. The option that you choose depends on the space that you have available, the amount of jewelry that you have and the type of jewelry you need to store. More expensive jewelry is best stored in closed storage to protect the precious metals and jewels, whereas costume jewelry can be kept more visible and remain out in the open.

In order to avoid tangles, I prefer to hang my necklaces, and just have a simple display set up using an inexpensive set of wall hooks. A ceramic egg holder works well to sort out my rings, and a tiered jewelery organizer holds my bracelets. While it's not very fancy, it allows me to see everything at one glance, provides quick access to whatever I would like to wear and is very easy to maintain.

Organize the Bedside Tables

The last thing that you want to have beside you when you're trying to have a peaceful sleep is a big pile of clutter, so take some time to clear off your night table and organize the area around your bed. Your night table should be reserved exclusively for items that you use right before bed, will need first thing in the morning when you wake up or may need during the night. Any other items that you need to keep should be stored elsewhere.

Take everything off of the tops of your night tables and give them a good dusting and wipe down. Add your necessities back first, such as a table light, phone or clock and then decide what other items might be helpful for you. For example, if you take your jewelry off right before bed, you may want to place a decorative tray on your table to hold these items. If you always need a drink of water in the middle of the night, you may want a pretty carafe. Choose just a couple of items that you love and get rid of all of the extras that are weighing it down.

If you also have drawers or a bottom storage area in your night table, empty and clean these as well. Use drawer dividers or small containers to provide a specific location for all of the little items that you may store in your drawer, like beauty products that you use right before bed, medications that may be needed in the night or any current books that you are reading. Remember that this space is for regularly used items only—get rid of those items that you do not use, love and need to access from your bed.

Organize the Bed Linens

You likely don't spend a lot of time thinking about your linens, but they are actually one of the most used items in the house. Since you use them for seven or eight hours every day, purchase quality sets that you can enjoy. While some people have a separate linen closet in their home, I like to store our bedroom linens in the bedroom where they are used. A storage ottoman, bench or trunk at the end of the bed is a great place for this, but if this is not available you can also store them under the bed (a crate similar to the DIY Under the Bed Storage Tray on page 126 would work well), in a dresser drawer or in the master closet.

Before we get started with organizing the bed linens, take a look at how you're dressing your bed. Do you like having a lot of pillows or do they just seem like extra weight to you? Do you actually use all of the sheets on your bed or do you just have them there because you're supposed to? Your bed should be your retreat at the end of a long day, so use whatever makes you comfortable and happy. If you like to use a lot of pillows on your bed and you take the time to make it each day (or almost every day) then the pillows are probably worth their weight. If, however, you rarely make your bed and the extra pillows just sit on the floor all the time, they are likely something that you should let go. For me, I never use a flat sheet on our bed—it always ended up being bunched at the bottom every morning and it made it a lot more difficult to make the bed. We now just use a fitted sheet and washable duvet cover and, as a result, I'm more comfortable at night and the bed always gets made.

When you are sorting through your linens, keep only those items that you actually use and love, and decide how many sheet sets you really need. Do you use lighter cotton sheets for summer and prefer heavier or flannel sheet sets for winter, or do you use the same style all year round? If you use the same style, you should really only need a couple of sets—one that is currently on your bed and one change. If you like to change things out seasonally, you may want to keep an extra set or two, but make sure that you have the space available somewhere for storage.

I store our sheets folded up and placed in one of the pillowcases that it belongs with. This keeps all of the items together and neatly stored. Taking the time to properly fold your sheets not only helps to reduce wrinkles in the sheets, but also takes up less space than poorly folded, jumbled sheets. The fitted sheet can be a little bit tricky to fold correctly (I think it took me a good half an hour to first figure it out!) but once you've done it a few times, it really only takes about a minute or two to complete.

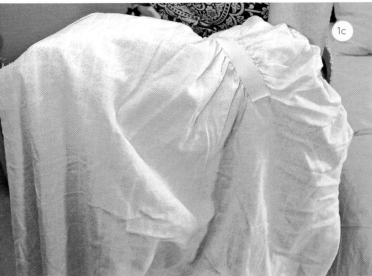

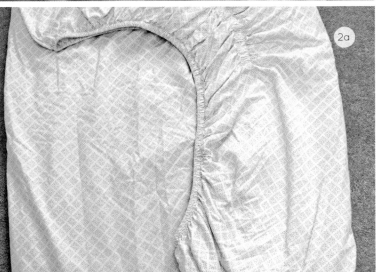

Long Side of Sheet
Wrong Side of Sheet Facing Out

How to Fold a Fitted Sheet

The smaller and thinner the sheet is that you are folding the easier it will be, so start by practicing on a twin sheet if you have one. Gently shake out and smooth your sheets after each step to keep your sheet from getting tangled up. The task of folding a fitted sheet can be divided into two main parts—gathering all of the corners together (which I do standing) and folding up the sheet (which I do on a flat surface).

Step 1: Gather the Corners

Throughout this step, think of your left hand as the holding hand and your right hand as the working hand.

a. With the sheet inside out (back side facing out), tuck one hand in each of the corners lengthwise along the sheet.

b. Bring your right hand toward your left hand and flip the corner of the sheet from your right hand over your left hand so the corners match up. Your left hand should now be holding the two corners.

c. Cross your right arm over your left and run your right hand down the elastic until you come to the next corner. Grab this corner and flip it over the left hand again like you did with the first corner. The corner that's showing will be inside out.

d. Bring the last corner up and flip it over your left hand again so it envelops the other corners. It should have the right side showing (not be inside out).

Step 2: Fold the Sheet

a. Lay the folded sheet on a flat surface and smooth it out into almost a rectangle shape with the elastic sides folded inward.

b. Fold the sheet lengthwise into thirds and smooth down.

Fold the sheet widthwise into thirds and smooth down.

Tips to Maintain a Healthy Weight in the Master Bedroom

- Do a quick closet clean-up every month, making sure that everything is in its proper spot. This reinforces your organization system and allows you to stay on top of any areas that are starting to get cluttered.

- Keep a donation box handy so you can place any items in it immediately if you decide that you no longer like the item or that it no longer fits you.

- Review all of your clothing items and accessories at the end of every season. If you did not wear or use an item during the current season, donate it rather than packing it away. As you take items out of storage to hang in your closet, try on any items that you are unsure about and donate anything that doesn't fit or you no longer like.

- Follow the "calories in and calories out" rule and donate an old item if you purchase something similar.

- Sort through all of your socks and undergarments twice per year, tossing items that are worn or stretched and making note of what new items you need to purchase.

CHAPTER 9
SLENDERIZING THE HOME OFFICE

· ·

While you may not have a dedicated room for your home office, you should have an area of your home somewhere where you have some sort of desk space and storage for your important paperwork. Keeping your office space clear of clutter helps you to focus and be more efficient with your work, and developing an organization system for your papers makes it much easier to keep up with all of your bill payments and other responsibilities.

I find that the best time to organize the office is around tax time, as you need to go through a lot of your paperwork anyway to prepare for your upcoming taxes, and your financial situation is pretty much staring you right in the face. Depending on how easy it was for you to find all of your tax information, you should know exactly what is and what isn't working for you in regard to your filing system and general office organization.

Shedding the Pounds

While paperwork is often the biggest source of weight in the home office (and often overflows into other areas of the house as well!), electronic gadgets, office supplies and home office equipment can also quickly add up. Take some time to trim things down as much as possible as you work through your home office space. Less weight results in a more efficient space for you to get your work done so you will have more time to play!

PENS, MARKERS, HIGHLIGHTERS—Check all pens to make sure that they are still working well and toss all that are running out of ink or are in a color that you won't use. Pens can be one of those items that you end up collecting way too many of, so donate any extras to a school or charity.

PENCILS—Toss any pencils that are almost at their end. Ensure that you have a pencil sharpener (or extra lead for mechanical pencils) and proper erasers stored in the same location.

SMALLER OFFICE SUPPLIES—Sort through all of your basic office supplies such as paper clips, elastic bands and push pins, and toss what you will not use. These should be stored in small containers or compartments to keep them organized.

STAPLERS—Ensure that your stapler is working properly and that you have staples stored close by. You should really only need one working stapler, so keep your favorite and get rid of the rest.

BUSINESS CARDS—As you are going through your office space, place any business cards that you find in one spot. Go through all of these at the end and toss out those that you no longer need. Store the remaining cards in a business card organizer or in a binder with plastic card dividers.

ELECTRONICS—Go through all of your electronic devices and recycle or donate any items that you no longer use. For those items that you're keeping, ensure that you have all of the charging cords labeled that go with them.

CORDS AND WIRES—The home office can be full of an array of cords. Ensure that you know where all of your cords lead or what devices they attach to and label them accordingly with washi tape, colored wire ties or another color-coded system. Go wireless when possible.

PAPERWORK—Gather up all paperwork and decide what items you no longer need. Shred any papers with personal information on them and recycle.

NOTEBOOKS/POST-IT NOTES—While notebooks and Post-it notes can be a great thing, sometimes you just have way too many! Keep only what you need and consider giving the rest to a school or other association that could use them. If you have separate planners for work and personal use, consider combining these into one and using a color-coding system instead to separate work from personal information.

PLANNERS—Recycle or shred any out-of-date planners. Only keep current planners if you use them and find them helpful. Personally, I still love written planners to keep myself organized, but if you prefer to use your phone or other technology for this, let go of your paper planners.

CALENDARS—Recycle any old calendars. If there are photos in the calendar that you really like, cut them out and add them to a photo frame to display. If you have multiple current calendars, pick your favorite and recycle the others.

OTHER ITEMS—Return all items that you would like to keep but don't belong in the office area to wherever they belong. Put them away immediately.

Building Strength: Exercises for the Home Office

To organize your home office and keep all of your paperwork under control, you must have a solid plan in place. Your home office space holds a lot of vital information—personal documents, important files such as taxes, financial records—and these all need to be safely stored and easily accessible for when you need them. This section guides you through a series of exercises to develop systems for controlling your paper weight and keeping all of your home office supplies and equipment organized and functional.

Regardless of whether you have a separate home office or just a small area dedicated to office duties, you still want to work on dividing the space into the functional zones that you would like. Those of you with small spaces may only need a couple of zones, while bigger spaces can be used for a much wider range of functions. If you have a whole room, you may want to create a zone for craft and hobby use or somewhere for your children to use as a homework area or art station (see page 138 for more details on this). If you work from home, you should have a separate zone for your work storage and personal storage. Keep your chosen zones in mind as you work through the following tasks.

Organize the Desk and Office Space

It can be really difficult to focus on your work when your desk and other office spaces are disorganized and you have to pause every few minutes to look for something that you need. Take some time to organize your space the way you like it and make sure that all of the items that you use regularly are within easy reach. Some of you may only have a desk to organize in this exercise while others will have a whole room. Either way, the steps are the same—you may just have a few extra functional zones to work on.

Step 1: Start with a Clean Slate

Empty your desk and sort the items into similar groupings as you go, such as notebooks, pens/pencils, small office supplies, paperwork, electronics and accessories. Decide which items you are keeping and sort the remaining items into toss, donate or belongs elsewhere. Ensure that any paperwork with personal information is shredded before recycling. Assess everything that you have decided to keep. Do you need, love and use everything? If not, shed a little more weight and get rid of these items. Wipe down the empty drawers and desktop. If your drawers are significantly marked or you just want a fun pop of color, line them with drawer liners (or make your own DIY Drawer Liners as outlined on page 98).

Step 2: Get All of Your Essentials Together

Finish sorting all of your keep items into the categories that you have chosen above. Determine what supplies are your most used items and decide how these should best be organized to make them easily accessible to you. Create some DIY Drawer Dividers (see page 101) or purchase a drawer organization unit to divide larger drawers into smaller, more functional subsections. This gives each category of items its own place and allows you to keep things more organized.

More frequently used items such as pens and pencils can also be stored in canning jars or other storage units on your desktop, but keep these items to a minimum to allow ample workspace and avoid a cluttered-looking desk. Make a designated home for your smaller electronic devices as well and keep all units and cords in one location.

Step 3: Get Creative with Your Storage

If you find that you have more office supplies and equipment than your current storage space allows (even after you have decluttered as much as possible), start thinking of other storage solutions that may meet your needs. If your desk surface is big enough, look for desktop organizers that can sit on top of your desk space. These can contain drawers, a space for file folders and additional storage for basic office supplies. To keep your workspace clear, look for metal rolling carts that can be placed just beside or underneath your desk. You can also think of going vertical and adding a wall-mounted shelf or two above your desk space.

For smaller items such as paper clips and push pins, repurpose ice cube trays or muffin tins in one of your desk drawers. I have a little egg cup on my work desk that's the perfect size for storing paper clips, so play around with what you've already got. If your drawers are deep enough, you can look at stackable drawer organizers to double the space available. Just remember to store your most used items on top and keep the bottom unit for less frequently used items.

For those of you who have a lot of supplies, or if you use your office for other functions such as craft storage, cube units are an inexpensive way to organize a wide variety of objects. Each cube can be used for different items and smaller drawers and cubbies can be used inside each cube if you have smaller items to store. Large filing boxes often fit perfectly into the cube spaces and these are easy to label so you know where everything is. The cube units themselves can also be arranged in a variety of ways to best meet your storage needs. Place them horizontally to allow extra workspace on top, or stack vertically to optimize storage in a smaller area.

If none of these options will work, look at storing less frequently used items elsewhere in your home, but keep them all together in one location so you will always know where they are.

Step 4: Add Personality

Once you have all of the essentials arranged, you can add a couple of decorative items to help your space feel more inspirational. Pretty calendars or clocks are a great way to add character while still being functional. You can also look for beautiful stationery or inspirational quotes, prints or special photos to display. Look for cork boards to hang above your desk space to temporarily hold papers, receipts, photos or other memorabilia, or use chalkboards or whiteboards to write down to-do lists or other ideas that you would like to follow through on.

DIY Drawer Liners

Drawer liners are a great way to add some new life, color and personality to old, scuffed drawers or cupboards. While you can purchase ready-made drawer liners in stores, these can be quite expensive and you often have to purchase more than you need. In addition, the patterns and colors available can be quite limited. Choosing this DIY option lets you customize your drawer liners to your unique style and can often be done with wrapping paper or scrapbook paper that you already have on hand.

Tape measure

Patterned or colored wrapping paper, scrapbook paper, etc.

Ruler

Scissors, craft knife or rotary cutter

Contact paper or clear adhesive vinyl

Clear decoupage gloss or double-sided tape (optional)

Step 1: Measure and Cut Wrapping Paper

Using a tape measure, measure the dimensions of the drawer or cupboard shelf that you are lining. Mark out the measurements on the back side of the wrapping paper and cut it to fit. Many papers have grid lines on the back that you can follow to keep your cutting line straight, but if not, be sure to use a ruler to mark a straight line before you start cutting. If you have an oversized cutting mat, you could use a ruler and a craft knife or rotary cutter to make this step even easier. Once you have cut out the paper, try it out in the drawer to make sure it fits. Trim if necessary.

Step 2: Cut the Contact Paper

I like to cut the contact paper about an inch or two (2 to 4 cm) bigger (both width and lengthwise) than the wrapping paper and then trim it down afterward. This gives me a little bit of wiggle room so it doesn't need to be lined up exactly with the paper. If you don't have any extra room available on the contact paper, you need to be careful that you accurately line it up when placing it over the top of your paper.

Step 3: Place the Contact Paper Over the Wrapping Paper

This step works easiest if you are working on a hard surface. Peel back a couple of inches of the contact paper backing and apply it to the patterned side of your paper. Once you have it positioned correctly, just continue to peel back the wrapper and unroll it over your paper until you are done. Trim the contact paper down where needed. You can always leave a slight edge on the contact paper to help prevent the paper from wiggling.

(continued)

DIY Drawer Liners (continued)

Step 4: Trim Off the Liner

Place the liner in the drawer. If there are any areas that the liner is too large, crease it against the side of the drawer edge and use craft knife to trim any excess.

Step 5: Adhere the Liner to Your Drawer Bottom (Optional)

If the measurements are done correctly and the liner fits well, I've found that I really don't need to adhere the paper down, especially if it is a small drawer. If you are lining a larger area, notice that your liner is sliding around or starting to roll at the edges, or have little ones that may try to pull it up, adding some adhesive is recommended. For a more removable adhesive, use double-sided poster tape in the corners and along the edges of the liner. For a more permanent adhesive, you can apply clear decoupage gloss to the drawer bottom before placing the liner on top and smoothing it down with a credit card.

DIY Drawer Dividers

Dividing up your drawer space into smaller functional units really helps to keep things organized and easy to find. While there are a lot of good pre-made versions on the market, these don't always fit your drawer space well or provide you with the divisions that you are looking for. This inexpensive DIY option lets you customize your dividers into any arrangement that you would like and can be done in any sized drawer. Don't limit these to the home office— think of the kitchen, bathroom, desk, bedside table, dressers and more!

Painter's tape (or masking tape)

Paint or stain (if desired)

¼-inch (6-mm) hobby board

Miter saw or handsaw

Sanding block

Clear heavy-duty wood glue (The glue will run over a bit, so make sure it dries clear so you won't see it.)

Step 1: Empty Out and Clean the Drawers

Empty the drawer. Wipe down the sides and bottom of the drawer.

Step 2: Design the Layout

Sort your keep items into categories. In this example, I was creating drawer dividers to sort our kitchen towels into washcloths, dishcloths, cleaning cloths, etc. Mark out in the drawer how you would like dividers spaced using painter's tape. Cut the tape so it is similar in width to the boards for a more accurate fit. Make sure everything fits. You might have to do a little playing around with this to make sure everything fits, especially if you're arranging a lot of little items.

Step 3: Paint or Stain if Desired

If you would like to paint or stain the wood, I found that it's easiest to do before you cut it. You can see photos of the painted drawer dividers on page 105. You will need to do a few touch-ups after the cutting, but it's much easier to handle one long board for painting than a bunch of small pieces. If you're going to be doing multiple drawers, just paint all of your boards at the same time. It will save you a lot of time in the long run.

Step 4: Cut the Boards

Measure the tape dividers that you have outlined in the drawer and cut down your hobby board to match. If you do not have the tools for this, you can likely get your pieces cut at the home building store when you purchase your boards. Double check that the boards fit by placing them back in the drawer. Sand down any rough edges.

(continued)

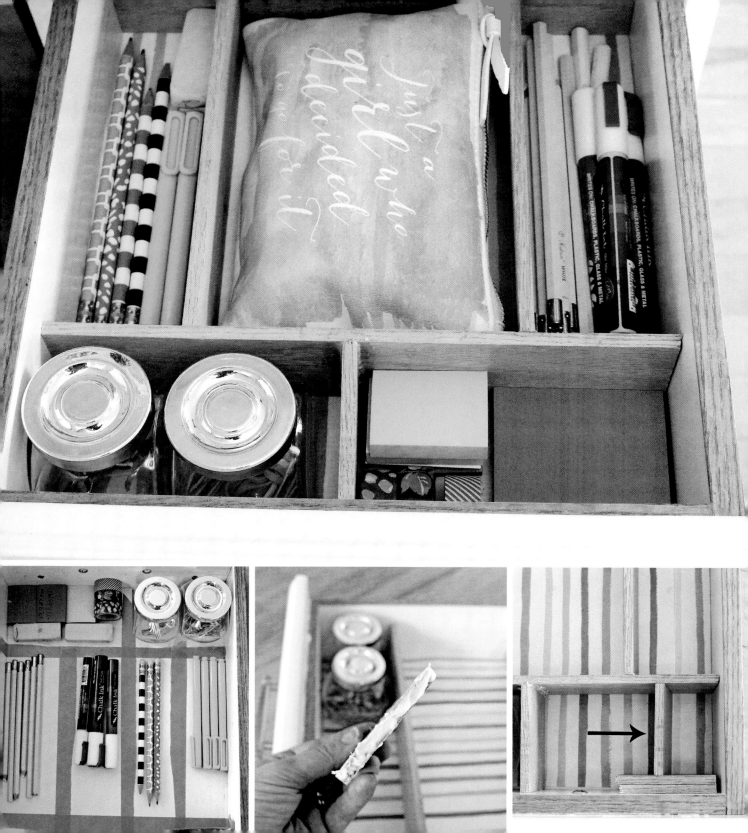

DIY Drawer Dividers (continued)

Step 5: Glue the Boards Together

Line your drawer with old paper or newspaper, if desired, to prevent the divider from sticking. Apply glue to the joints and press together. Remove excess glue with a toothpick or piece of cardboard. You may need to use scrap pieces of wood to stabilize the dividers in place when drying to ensure a solid bond (see bottom right image). Do not glue the pieces to the drawer itself so you can remove the divider for cleaning or to change the lay out. Allow the glue to dry completely.

Step 6: Replace the Items

Remove the newspaper from the base of the drawer. If you would like to line your drawers with drawer liner (DIY Drawer Liners on page 98) add this now. Put your drawer divider back in the drawer and arrange all of your items.

DIY Charging Station

We have quite a few electronic devices in our home and I was getting tired of having charging cables lying around everywhere. I also like to keep the kids' devices out of their bedrooms at night so I wanted to come up with a central place in our home that we could charge and store everything in one spot. While I ended up using a drawer for this project, you could also create a similar idea with a wooden desk storage unit or filing unit that could sit out on your desk, which would actually be simpler to create. The hobby board comes in a variety of widths, so you can choose the width that best suits your drawer size. You will have to measure your drawer to determine how much 1 x 2 and hobby board you will need.

Tape

1 x 2 boards

Paint or stain (optional)

¼-inch (6-mm) hobby board

Wood glue

Saw

Jigsaw or coping saw

1¼ inch (3 cm) screws

Drill with large drill bit

Power bar with extra-long cord

Step 1: Design the Layout
Gather up any electronics or related electronic products that you will store in the charging station and plan out where each item will go. You may not necessarily need to have all of your devices charging at the same time so just make sure that there is room for what you need. Use tape to mark out the divider locations.

Step 2: Paint or Stain the Wood Boards
If you would like to paint your boards, I found that it was easier to paint the boards prior to cutting them. If you're painting you will likely need a couple of coats (or use a primer and paint). Staining your boards with wood stain is another option.

Step 3: Frame Out the Sides of the Drawer (Optional)
Measure the drawer and cut the hobby boards to frame out the edges of the drawer. You can either use some clear wood glue to secure the boards together in a frame, or if you are accurate with your cuts, the boards will just stay in place through friction. While this step isn't completely necessary, it allows you to add rigidity to the system without having to permanently secure the dividers to the drawer itself. The whole system can then be removed easily for cleaning or if you no longer need it.

(continued)

Step 4: Cut the Divider Pieces

Using your tape design, determine the length that you need the dividers and cut your 1 x 2 boards using a saw. If you're not going to be using a frame around the drawer, make sure that the pieces that run the full length or width of the drawer fit snugly so the unit does not slide around within the drawer. Using a jigsaw or coping saw, cut out mouse holes in the dividers for cords to pass through.

Step 5: Screw the Divider Pieces Together

Test out the divider pieces in the drawer to make sure everything lines up and then screw the divider pieces together. Drill pilot holes to prevent any wood splitting.

Step 6: Line the Drawer (Optional)

If you would like to do a drawer liner to add some color or to cover up a worn drawer, add it now. See page 98 for instructions on a DIY liner. Once this is completed, add the divider unit back into the drawer.

Step 7: Add the Power Bar

Hang the power bar from the back of the drawer and drill a large hole through the back of the drawer and furniture unit so the cord can pass easily. Note: You will need to ensure that there is some space between the wall and your furniture piece to allow the cord to pass easily in and out of the hole as the drawer is opened and closed. The thinner the cord on the power bar, the easier this will be. You also want to make sure that there will be enough cord available to reach when the drawer is completely opened.

Step 8: Set Up the Devices

Keep some storage space for extra cords, power chargers and screen cleaners so all of your items are in one location. Use cord ties to coil up extra length of cord to keep everything tidy.

Organize a Family Command Center

A family command center is a central area in your home designed to organize your daily paperwork and family schedules—the one-stop location for you and your family to find calendars, information and messages that you need to stay on top of things each day. If you have difficulty controlling the paper clutter in your home and finding what you need to get out of the house on time each morning, creating (and using!) a family command center will go a long way in reducing your daily stress levels. There's no right way to create a command center as the needs of each family will vary, but there are a few basic steps to follow to get you up and running in no time.

Step 1: Choose the Location

A family command center can be set up anywhere that you like, but it's best to put it as close as possible to where you would typically drop your stuff when you come into your home. For many people this is the kitchen, front entry or mudroom. When choosing your location, look for spots where your clutter tends to accumulate and find a spot close by that works for you.

A family command center doesn't have to be anything fancy or take up a lot of space. It can be as simple as getting a three-ring binder with some dividers and a few pockets. Others like to use a wall space in their home where it's more visible to everyone. If you are short on space, look at using the inside of a cupboard door or closet or a little nook.

Step 2: Determine What You Need to Include

Spend some time thinking about what it is that you have difficulty keeping organized and what information needs to be shared. What types of things are you constantly looking for? What things are your family always asking you about? Answering these questions should help guide you in your decision of what to include, but here are a few common items that are often used in a family command center:

- Frequently called phone numbers and emergency contacts
- Shopping lists
- Coupon storage
- Personal files for each member of the family for short-term storage. This could include school forms that you will be returning, information on the current extra-curricular activities, etc. More long-term personal information such as medical cards or passports should be stored in your filing system which we will talk about later (on page 110).

- Incoming and outgoing mail
- Current bills to pay
- Takeout menus/flyers that you wish to follow up on
- Current receipts that you are keeping handy for returns, etc.
- Whiteboard or chalkboard for reminders or other notes
- Monthly calendar
- Storage for basic office supplies
- Charging station

Step 3: Organize Your Paperwork

Gather up all of your papers and sort them quickly into three piles: keep, recycle and shredding (for any paperwork that has personal information on it). Note that right now we'll be working with the papers that you use on a very regular basis. We'll be dealing with organizing your other important paperwork later on in the exercises, so you can just place any of these into a to-file folder to get them out of the way for now. Group the papers from the keep pile into categories that make sense to you. This can include (but is definitely not limited to):

- Bills to pay
- Upcoming events
- Kids' papers
- Coupons
- Records to file and papers that need to be kept long-term
- Personal papers for each person in your household

Create a designated spot for each of these categories. You can use a portable file system, wall mounted files, a three-ring binder or anything else that will work for you. I use both wall mounted files as well as a small drawer unit that's kept by our phone, so mix and match to find whatever suits your needs.

Step 4: Put It All Together

Once you have decided how you want your family command center to look, you can determine what items you can use that you already have in your home and what items you may need to purchase. Remember that you are trying to cut down on clutter, so only purchase what you will need and use. It may take a few weeks of using the system to really figure out how it will work for you, so start with the basics and add more if needed.

Develop a Paper Trail

Paperwork can be a huge source of stress for many people, and it can be very overwhelming when it comes to trying to organize it all. It's amazing how quickly all of that paper can add up, so it's extremely important that you have a plan in place for how to organize it. Creating this paper trail helps you come up with an organization system that works for you and banishes that paper clutter once and for all.

Step 1: Determine Location of Current Paper Dumping Ground

In order to tackle all of your paperwork (and develop a long-term plan to keep it organized), you need to have an idea of where it comes from, where it goes when it enters your home and where it should ultimately end up. First you need to figure out where your common dumping ground is. This is the place that you would typically drop your mail or other papers when you first bring it into your home.

Step 2: Set Up a Primary Paper Organization Center

To stick with an organization system, it needs to be simple, it needs be convenient and it needs to be practical. Now that you know where your natural dumping ground for your papers tends to be, set up your organization system as close to this as possible or choose another convenient location. If you have already set up a family command center (see page 107), you may already have done this step. You don't need to have anything fancy—a portable filing box, some file folders attached to the inside of your cabinet doors or a small, wall-mounted filing system all work well. This primary paper organization center should always be the first landing spot for any papers coming into your home and should be used for short-term paper storage only. From this location, you can then sort your papers into the categories that will determine what the next plan of action will be.

I have four main categories that I use to sort my paperwork in this short-term storage area and use a file folder to organize each of them. One is for coupons and gift cards, one is for bills to pay, one is for things to do (these are items that require some action—forms to fill out, an appointment that needs to be made, a letter that requires mailing) and one is for things to file (these are things that need to be filed in our long-term storage such as financial records and tax information). I also have a set of small drawers below that I use for the kids' school papers. You can use whatever categories make sense for you—think about what types of papers you deal with on a regular basis and what things you currently have trouble keeping organized.

Step 3: Gather Loose Papers and Sort Into Categories

Gather up any loose papers that you can find from around the house and quickly sort them into three piles: keep, recycle (or garbage) and shred (for any paperwork that has any personal information on it). Take all of the items from your keep pile and place them into the appropriate files that you set up in the previous step. If there are additional paper items that don't really fit any of your files, you may need to add more files or adjust your categories.

Step 4: Complete Your Paper Trail

Schedule some time each week to complete your paper trail—if this is done regularly it really shouldn't take that long. Papers in your to-do file should be completed and sent back out the door. Papers in your to-file folder should be taken down to your long-term storage and filed appropriately, and any bills in your bills to pay file should be paid. Take a couple of minutes to go through everything remaining and see if there are any items that can be tossed or were missed. If you can, pick a set day of the week to do this and stick with your schedule.

By using this system, all paperwork should be limited to one of two areas in your home—your short-term paper storage area and your long-term paper storage which we will be talking about next. You need a plan and an end destination for every piece of paper that comes into your home. Once you have everything set up and organized, dedicate 10 to 15 minutes one day per week to maintaining your system.

Organize Personal Records

Throughout the years, we end up gathering a wide variety of important personal records from birth certificates and medical cards to banking information and house records. By setting up your paper trail, you should now have an efficient method of sorting and organizing your papers as they come into your home. This section focuses on how to organize your personal records that should be kept in your long-term filing system.

Step 1: Gather Up All of Your Papers

Gather up any pieces of personal paperwork if it's not already stored in one location and take anything from your short-term paper storage that you had wanted to file. Quickly sort through your pile of papers. Toss any obvious junk into the garbage and shred any papers with personal information that you no longer need. Take some time to go through your remaining papers to ensure that you really need to keep everything that you have left. If information is outdated, duplicated elsewhere or can easily be retrieved online, get rid of it!

Step 2: Set Up a Filing System

Depending on your needs, your filing system can be anything from a small, portable filing box to a larger, dedicated filing cabinet. Choose the smallest system possible that works for you. Sort all of your remaining paperwork into categories, avoiding the dangerous miscellaneous category that can quickly accumulate clutter. While this list isn't exhaustive, the categories may include:

CREDIT CARDS—Keep one year of statements (if they are not available online) and your credit card agreement information. Ensure that you have your credit card numbers written out and the phone number that you need to call if your card is lost or stolen. If you need your credit card statements for tax purposes, these will be transferred to your tax records when you file your taxes. If you don't need them for taxes, shred your statements after one year.

HOUSE AND AUTOMOBILE INSURANCE—Keep all current records. Shred the old insurance record when a new one is received after you have verified that all of the new information is correct.

MORTGAGE AGREEMENT—Shred any old agreements and keep only your most recent one.

INVESTMENT INFORMATION—Compare new statements to your old ones. If there are no discrepancies, shred the outdated copies.

BANK STATEMENTS AND ACCOUNT INFORMATION—For the most part, bank statements are readily available online so discontinue your monthly paper statements unless you need them for tax purposes. Keep all account numbers and passwords on file.

MEDICAL AND DENTAL INSURANCE—Keep current copies only.

PAYSTUBS AND OTHER WORK INFORMATION—While I generally just keep the most updated paystub, you can keep them for up to one year if you find that you actually need to refer back to them. These can be shredded when you have received your income tax records from your employer and all of the information has been verified.

TAX INFORMATION—You can either choose to keep your tax information stored in one file throughout the year or file information away by category such as medical receipts, investment information and charitable donations. I like to store my tax information in a separate portable filing unit instead of with the rest of my long-term paperwork and sort it into the appropriate categories as I receive it throughout the year. It's then all ready to be taken to our tax accountant at the end of the year.

PERSONAL FILE FOR EACH FAMILY MEMBER—Keep a current photo of each family member labeled with their height and weight as well as other personal information such as birth certificates, passports and medical records.

WARRANTIES AND IMPORTANT RECEIPTS—Sort through this regularly to see what you no longer need to keep. Look for warranties that have expired or paperwork for items that you no longer have.

Step 3: Start Filing

Label your file folders according to the categories that you have come up with above. You may also choose to color code your system or organize your files alphabetically. File all papers into the appropriate categories.

You may also wish to purchase a fireproof box or rent a bank safety deposit box to ensure that documents like marriage and birth certificates, wills, passports, valuable contracts, citizenship papers, a computer hard drive with photos or other important information are kept safe.

Organize Finances

Organizing your finances can go a long way in improving financial health and decreasing stress levels. Late fees, bad credit ratings and a high debt load can quickly result if you don't have a plan in place to keep things organized and running smoothly. Creating a family budget is essential to know where all of your money is going each month and to determine where you might be able to find some ways to cut your spending if needed.

Step 1: Gather Up All of Your Financial Records and Bills

If you have already organized your personal records, it should be easy to find all of your financial records and bills. Ensure that you have all of your monthly bills (or can find them online) as well as have access to your past bank records (either online or on a paper statement) for at least the past month.

Step 2: Write Out a Monthly Budget

Write out all of your monthly income sources and any monthly expenses. There are many pre-made forms that you can find online to help keep track of your income and expenses or you can always choose to write up your own list or create a digital document in a spreadsheet. Mark your expenses as either a fixed expense (mortgage, car payment, insurance that are the same every month) or a controllable expense (food, entertainment, personal care). If your budget is not looking too healthy, you will want to look at cutting back on your controllable expenses as much as possible. Your fixed expenses should ideally be no more than 50 to 60 percent of your total take-home pay. If you are not exactly sure what you spend each month (and since spending can vary from month to month), you may want to keep a more detailed analysis of what you are spending over a three- to six-month period.

When you are developing your budget, don't forget about including a savings plan. Even starting with a small amount can add up over time and will help to get you in the routine of saving. Make sure you are contributing to some kind of long-term savings account or investment funds. If you have kids, start a college fund as early as possible and look for government plans that will contribute money to this as well.

Step 3: Develop a System for Paying Your Bills

Creating a regular routine for paying your bills, as well as a way to track what bills have and haven't been paid, is very important when it comes to organizing your finances. We will be taking a closer look at this in the next section. Keep your monthly budget stored in the same location that you pay your bills or keep these all together in a family financial binder.

Organize Bill Payments

Late bill payments can lead to extra fees, a poor credit rating and a whole lot of unnecessary stress. By developing a specific system to pay your bills, you can make this process much simpler and ensure that you get those bills paid on time every month.

Step 1: Gather Up All of Your Bills

Gather up all of your paper bills and decide where you are going to keep them. If you are not going to keep them where you actually pay your bills, make sure that you store them in a portable file or basket so they are easy to transport. Throughout the week, I file mine away in our kitchen command center and then take them down to our home office area in the basement when I am ready to pay them. For those bills that you receive electronically, create a separate bill folder in your email inbox to keep all of your bill notification emails. This ensures that they don't get lost in your mass of emails and will serve as a reminder to pay them. Delete them once they have been paid. You may want to keep one email from each of your monthly online bills so that you can easily access your account whenever you would like.

Step 2: Write Out a List of All Your Regular Monthly Bill Payments

Having a list of all of your regular monthly bill payments helps you stay on top of things and ensures that you are not forgetting anything. These can either be written out by hand or done electronically on your computer. There are also a number of printable bill trackers available online that can be downloaded and used for this.

Generally you have two types of bill payments each month—those that you have set up to be withdrawn automatically from your bank account and those that you have to actually pay manually (either online or through the mail). Write down your automatic payments and when they are withdrawn on one list and create a second list for the payments that you have to pay manually and when those payments are due. When you are first setting up your lists, go through your bank statement from the previous month to ensure that you have not left anything out.

Step 3: Create a Space Where You Will Regularly Pay Your Bills

If you don't have a home office or other designated desk space, come up with another place in your home that will work. You'll need to make sure that you have your lists of bill payments and access to a computer as well as any basic home office supplies that may be needed (pens, calculator, envelopes, stamps). Keep these items all together in a small zippered pouch or other container.

Step 4: Create a Designated Bill Payment Time

Schedule some time in your regular routine for bill paying. I pay ours every Friday, but you could set a schedule for every payday or other set time that works for you. If you are not paying your bills on a weekly basis, schedule in some time at least once per week to check your bank accounts for automatic bill payments that may be coming out. Check off your bills as you pay them each month, what amount you paid and which day you completed the payment.

Tips to Maintain a Healthy Weight for the Home Office

- Keep a file folder on your desk and/or at your family command center labeled "To-File." Place any papers that need to be added to your filing system in this folder during the week and then file them all away at one time once the week is over.

- Get rid of junk mail as soon as it enters the house. Cancel catalogs and magazine subscriptions that you don't really read and take yourself off mailing lists.

- Follow the "one touch" rule as much as possible. Once you touch a piece of paper, either act upon it immediately, file it in the appropriate place or throw it away/shred it. Keep extra file folders on hand in case you need to start a new file category that you hadn't thought of.

- Go paperless as much as possible. Set up your credit card statements, banking information and bill payments on line so these are not mailed to you every month. Create a separate folder in your email account to put your online monthly statements until they are paid so your bills don't get lost in your emails. If you do require this information for tax purposes, be sure to print out any information needed each month and file them away in your tax folder.

- Frequently review your budget and make any necessary changes. If your budget is relatively stable you can do this every three to four months; however, if you are just getting started on your budget or really working on improving your financial health, do this monthly. Do a full budget update annually.

- Have a designated day each week for filing and paying bills. Ten to fifteen minutes per week usually does it for me and sticking to this avoids those paper mounds piling up!

- Do a quick tidy of your desk space and surrounding area each month, tossing out any items that are no longer needed, recycling old paperwork and ensuring that all of your items are in their proper place.

- Periodically review your filing system and adapt your categories as needed. Have a file that rarely gets used? Combine that info into another file folder. Is a file bulging at the seams? Check to see if everything in there is needed and if it is, create subcategories either by date or topic.

- Restrict all paperwork to their dedicated areas only: short-term command center paper storage or long-term storage area. Do not let them invade your other spaces!

CHAPTER 10

PARING DOWN THE KIDS' ROOMS

· ·

Anyone who has had kids knows that their stuff can quickly take over a whole house. Not only is this overwhelming for you, but it can also be very overwhelming for your children. Having your kids' items limited to specific areas of the house makes it easier for them to find what they are looking for and learn how to organize and care for their own belongings.

I like to work on organizing the kids' rooms just before back-to-school time as I need to go through their clothing and school supplies anyway to prepare for the upcoming school year. After a summer at home with lots of time to play, it also gives me a good idea of what toys are still being used and what toys they have grown out of. I feel that kids should be included in the organization process as much as possible when it comes to sorting and organizing their own belongings and find that this helps them participate in keeping things tidy and organized in the long run. Working on their spaces over summer vacation provides the time needed to spend on these areas without feeling rushed.

· ·

Shedding the Pounds

When it comes to accumulating clutter, nothing seems to grow faster than kids' items! The needs and interests of young children especially can change so quickly that it can be hard to keep up with all of the weight gain. The younger your children are, the more frequently you need to sort through and purge old items that are no longer used. If you plan on saving your child's items for future children or for hand-me-downs, be sure to only keep your best items and only what you need. If you do keep these items, be sure to sort through them all before purchasing new items for the younger child to avoid duplicates.

Kids' items can also be the hardest items to let go of emotionally as there are so many wonderful memories that go along with them. As you are sorting through the items, remember that the memories are not actually attached to the object and will not disappear if you let the object go. You can always take a photo of the item and write a little note on the back of it or create a scrapbook page of favorite items if you are finding this process hard. While we can't keep everything, there may be some extremely special items that you will want to hold on to like a favorite stuffed animal or blanket, the first outfit worn home from the hospital or special keepsakes. Decide on a specific amount of room that you have for these objects (such as one plastic storage bin) and restrict the items to that space only.

CLOTHING—Sort through all clothing and toss any items that are extremely worn or torn. Donate items that do not fit and have your children try on any clothing that you are not sure about. If you pick one shirt and one pair of pants that fit them well, you can use this as a guide to compare other clothing articles to so they don't have to try on their whole wardrobe.

SHOES—Go through all shoes and determine which items still fit and which items your kids actually wear. Sometimes kids can be picky with their shoe choices, so even if the shoes are in good condition, if your child won't actually wear them, there's no point in keeping them around. Donate items that are still in good condition and toss the rest. Looking at the soles of the shoes often gives you the best indication if they are still in good shape to sell or donate—if the tread is significantly worn off or if they are particularly worn on one side of the sole, it's best to toss them.

SPORTSWEAR—Go through all of your child's sports equipment and sportswear to see what still fits. If you're at the end of the season, assess whether it's still likely to fit in the next season and donate it if not. For equipment that's still in good shape, sell it or trade it in at second-hand sports stores for the next size up.

SEASONAL ITEMS—Winter gear especially can take up a lot of space, so be sure to store only what you will likely need when the season comes around again. Donate items that will be too small or that you have duplicates of. If you are tight on space, store seasonal clothing items that you will be keeping elsewhere.

BOOKS—Books are wonderful for children, but having too many can make it overwhelming for your child when choosing what books they want to read and finding their favorites in the huge stack. Keep your child's favorite books as well as a few books on hand for the next reading level, but donate the rest of the books that are no longer being read or loved.

TOYS—Toys should be sorted through frequently to keep the weight down. The younger your children, the more frequently this needs to be done. Toss any toys with broken or missing pieces that can no longer be used and donate other items that your kids no longer need or use. Involve your children in this process as much as possible, keeping their age and maturity level in mind. Having fewer toys can allow them to play more with the toys that they actually do have. Contain the toys to specific areas of the house.

STUFFED ANIMALS—Sort through all stuffies and toss or donate items that are no longer loved. Confine stuffed animals to a specific space such as a bin or basket to limit the collection to a reasonable amount. Only donate stuffed animals that are still in excellent condition.

DECOR ITEMS—While there are a ton of cute children's decor items on the market, be careful about going overboard with theme-related items. Children's likes can change quickly and you can be left with a pile of themed items that they no longer want.

ARTWORK AND SCHOOLWORK—Go through all of your children's artwork and schoolwork and keep only the pieces that have the most meaning to you—Mother's or Father's Day cards, artwork with funny sayings or pictures, items with little handprints or footprints, etc. While it may be tempting to keep everything, these items can really pack on the pounds fast over the years. Take photos of artwork that you would still like to remember, rather than keeping the actual piece. The photos can then be placed into a scrapbook or made into a photo book online. You will still be able to keep the memories without taking up the space!

ART SUPPLIES AND SCHOOL SUPPLIES—Art supplies can often take quite a beating at the hands of little children, so sort through everything to see what is still functional. Toss pens that have dried up or paints that have all mixed together and donate items in good condition that your child no longer uses. Often children just prefer simple crayons, colored markers and paper rather than the fancier art equipment and coloring books that are out on the market.

OTHER ITEMS—Return all items that you would like to keep but don't belong in the kids' rooms to wherever they belong.

Building Strength: Exercises for the Kids' Rooms

We all know that kids' rooms can go from clean to a disaster zone in less than 30 minutes. By developing a strong organization system, you will be much more prepared to deal with these messes, and cleaning up those disasters will be so much quicker and easier. Having an organized space for your children can also help them to increase their independence and learn important life skills that will benefit them down the road as well.

Include your children in the following exercises as much as possible and ask for their input when it comes to organizing their own spaces—you might be pleasantly surprised at what they come up with! Some kids will obviously be more interested in the process than others, but all can benefit from developing a few early organization skills.

Organize the Closets

I will say that we are very lucky when it comes to the bedroom closets in our home as they are all quite spacious and provide us with a lot of storage. All of the same principles and ideas still apply to smaller closets though, so use what you've got and optimize that space!

When it comes to kids' closets, the main goal is to make everything as visible and accessible to your children as possible. The more that they are able to do on their own the better! If you have the space, don't limit the closet to clothing items only—it can be a great place to store toys, stuffed animal collections or extra bedding to keep the main room as clutter-free as possible and provide a nice open area for play.

Step 1: Empty the Closet and Clean

Take everything out of the closet and sort the items into keep, try-on, donate, toss and belongs elsewhere piles. Once the closet is empty, vacuum or sweep the floor (especially into the corners) and wipe down or dust any shelving or furniture pieces.

Step 2: Sort the Keep Items

Have your child try on all of the clothing that you had placed in the try-on pile and keep those items that fit and that your child will wear. Children with sensory issues may be particular to specific clothing items, so give them some choice in what items they actually want to wear. Clothing battles are not usually worth the time and effort! Sort all of the remaining keep items into categories and re-assess once more for additional items to get rid of.

Step 3: Choose Your Storage Solutions

There are a number of storage possibilities when it comes to organizing the kids' closets. The way that you choose to organize your closet will be dependent on the age and maturity level of your child as well as the space that you have available. As with all closets, maximize all of the space available while still keeping those items that your children can use independently accessible and visible to them.

CLOSET RODS—While it may not be the most space-efficient method, hanging clothing from hangers is the simplest way to keep your child's clothing easily visible and is fairly low-maintenance. Since children's clothing is smaller, having both a lower rod and upper rod will definitely accommodate their clothing and the lower rod can make it much easier for children to access their most used items. If you use this method, teach your children how to hang up their own clothes as soon as they are old enough—it may take a couple of months of practice but is definitely a useful habit to learn. Another option is to use a hanging sweater bag to store clothes as an outfit. Each compartment can be used for a different day of the week to minimize morning fusses when it comes to choosing outfits.

BINS AND BASKETS—I love using bins in kids' spaces as they are easy for kids to use and visually keep the clutter away. Bins can be used to store clothing such as socks, underwear and pajamas that you don't have to worry about folding and arranging—just toss them in and go. I also like to keep a couple of extra baskets on the top shelf of the closet to store clothing items that don't fit—one bin is a donation bin for items that they have outgrown, and the other bin is for items that are still a little big for them. I don't like to store these too far away or I often forget about them until it's too late! Bins are also my favorite storage item for toys. They make clean-up a cinch and can be carted around the house if the kids want to play with them elsewhere.

MISCELLANEOUS FURNITURE PIECES—If you don't have any built-in shelving units in the closet, bookshelves or other furniture units that fit into the space can work great for providing extra storage. Paint mismatched second hand furniture the same color for an inexpensive, custom look.

LAUNDRY BASKETS—Laundry baskets can be used for more than storing dirty laundry! They work great for storing extra blankets or bedding and can serve as the perfect home for your child's stuffed animal collection. Both of my children love their stuffies and would have had a lot more if they had it their way. By limiting the collection to one laundry hamper, they can choose which ones they keep and know that no new ones are allowed unless there is space available in their basket.

HOOKS—Hooks are very practical in children's spaces as they can be hung at their level and are easy for little ones to access. Use these for frequently used items such as favorite hoodies, backpacks, hats or use to hang their outfit for the next day so they can easily get dressed in the morning.

Step 4: Add the Finishing Touches

Put all of your items back into their specific locations and show your child how everything is arranged—especially if there are toys in there! If you have the space, you can add a few decorative pieces such as a favorite poster or photo, sports mementos or a little chalkboard.

Organize the Drawers

Most kids' rooms have drawer storage somewhere in dressers, other storage units or in their nightstand tables. I find that drawer storage is the hardest method to maintain for kids, so I use it more for toys and bedding storage than for clothing. Even the most perfectly organized drawer can be dismantled by a child in two seconds!

Step 1: Empty Out the Drawer and Clean

Sort the items in the drawer into your decluttering categories as you empty them and clean out any dust, crumbs or other little items that make their way into the corners of the drawers. If the drawer is worn (or is colored with crayons all over the bottom!), you can add some DIY Drawer Liners (see page 98) to give it some new life.

Step 2: Divide Up the Space

If you have larger drawers, divide up the drawer space into smaller units by using DIY Drawer Dividers (see page 101), organization units or bins that fit the space. Bins work especially well for toy storage as they can be lifted out of the drawer and taken to the play area and they also make clean-up extremely easy. When storing items in a drawer, do not fill it up to capacity. If there's lots of extra space, your child will be able to access what they want without having to remove other items first.

Step 3: Replace the Items

Put the items back into the drawers, keeping the number of different categories in each drawer to a minimum. If you can just store one type of toy item in each drawer or one type of clothing item, it will be easier to maintain and find the items that you are looking for. Label the drawers if needed either with word labels or picture cards if your child can't yet read.

If you do store clothing items in drawers, keep it simple for younger children and have a specific drawer (or section of the drawer if you're using dividers) for each specific item. Young kids are not going to keep their clothes folded so you will likely need to put up with more of a toss-and-go method of organizing. As your kids get older and can manage to fold their clothes, use the vertical filing method to store clothes (see page 87) so that everything in the drawer remains visible and it's easy to remove one item without disturbing everything else.

Organize the Toys

For those of you with younger children, this will likely be the biggest category for you to organize. Between birthdays and holidays and grandparents visiting, your toy collection can seem to grow exponentially and can quickly take over the whole house. To make things even harder to keep organized, many items come with little parts and accessories that can easily get misplaced.

Before you even begin to start organizing, pare down the toys as much as possible. One of the things that I discovered when I was first organizing all of our kids' toys was that they really did not need or use probably half of what they had. There was so much extra weight! Here are a few tips and tricks that I have learned over the years to help keep our toy weight in check. Take a few minutes to read these over before you start sorting through your own toy collection.

Keep the Toys Limited to Specific Rooms or Areas

I know it can be difficult at times, but it is possible to not have toys in every room of your home. This tends to be harder to do when kids are younger and you always need to keep an eye on them when they are playing, but as your kids get older you can really start to narrow down the location of their toys to just a playroom or family room and their bedroom. If your younger children do have toys in more than one room, have some storage available in each space to make clean-up easier, and have the toys stay in the general area that they are stored.

Less is More

While it can be tempting to buy your children all of the latest toys on the market, think twice about whether or not they really need more toys and if they regularly play with them. Having fewer toys can actually be better for your children, as it allows them to stay more focused on the toys that they do have and encourages them to use more imaginative play. Introduce one new toy at a time to your child (especially younger children and toddlers) and really allow them to learn and explore that toy before adding more.

Look for Toys that Will Last

When you are purchasing toys for your children, think about what items your child will be likely to use over the long-term. Many toys have short-term appeal then quickly become old and just gather dust on the shelf. Look for toys that can be used in a variety of ways and require your children to use some imagination and creativity. Kids can also be rough on their toys, so choose higher-quality toys that are built to last.

Design Age-Appropriate Storage Systems

One of the main goals when organizing your children's toys is to make it easy for them to find, play with and hopefully put away whatever toys they choose. Place toys that are appropriate for them at a level where they can reach them, while keeping toys with little parts or those for older children only stored higher. Label all containers and work with your child to teach him to put items back in the correct bin. If they are old enough to understand this principle but don't yet read, use picture labels (either photographs of the actual object or a picture that you can print off of the computer) to label the containers.

Include Your Children in the Organization Process

The extent to which you include your child in this process will obviously be dependent on their age and maturity level, but include them as much as possible. I find that kids are more likely to stick with the routine if they have had some input into how their stuff is organized, and cleaning up after themselves and the importance of staying organized are helpful life skills. If you start working on these ideas at an early age, it becomes part of your child's regular routines and, over time, a lot less nagging and assistance will be required from you.

I've found that my kids are actually surprisingly good at deciding what items they want to keep and which items they no longer need. Unless they are holding on to items that obviously need to go, respect your child's choices and help them come up with ways that they can store those items that they have chosen to keep. Even quite young children can help to clean up their own toys, so encourage this practice early on and integrate clean-up time into your regular daily routine.

Think Outside of the (Toy) Box

There are many items around the house that can be used to entertain your children that are not specifically toys. If you are working on a house task and need to keep your child entertained while doing so, think of items that are readily available to you that your child might like. For example, if you are cooking dinner, maybe you can set up some plastic bowls or pots and pans with some wooden spoons for your little one to play with. My oldest son especially much preferred this over toys when he was little. If you frequently work in your office during the day, set up a little table beside your desk or in a corner for your child and give them some papers and crayons to draw with.

Rotate Your Toy Collection

If you have younger children, consider rotating toys so that everything is not available at once. Preschools do this quite frequently and often switch up their toys on a monthly basis to fit with different themes that they are working on. This can help to keep your child more interested in their toys and less overwhelmed with all of the choices available. Even old toys seem new again if they haven't seen them in a while! Of course, you don't have to switch out everything and can always keep your child's favorite things available to them; however, a few rotations here and there keeps things fresh and exciting while helping to cut down on the amount of mess that's made. Now that you have given the toys a little extra thought, it's time to get organizing!

Step 1: Gather Up the Toys

If you have toys in a variety of rooms (such as a playroom, family room and kid's bedroom), you can either organize them room by room or gather up all of the toys from around the house and organize them in your main toy storage area. If you have designated toys for designated rooms (for example the train set and board games are always in the playroom and the building bricks are always in the bedroom), it's fine to go room by room; however, if you find that you just have random toys spread all over the house, it really is best to gather them all up into one location.

Step 2: Sort the Toys

In addition to the regular keep, donate, toss and belongs elsewhere piles, have a bin to place random parts or pieces as you go along. You don't want to toss these pieces too early as you may find that you have a complete set once you have actually sorted through everything. Throw out any broken items, cheap toys from fast-food chains, and anything that is missing important parts once you have completely sorted through all of the toys. Donate items in good condition that your child no longer needs or plays with.

Sort the remaining keep items into categories such as board games, wooden toys, building toys or specific play sets. Once you have the toys categorized, look through the items one more time to see if there is any further weight that can be trimmed. Do your children really play with it all? Is it a reasonable amount of toys? Are there any duplicates that you can get rid of?

Step 3: Choose Storage Solutions

When it comes to children's spaces, it's nice to have a balance between closed storage and open storage solutions. Closed storage is nice to hide all of those random items and little pieces away and requires a lot less fuss to keep them looking organized. Open storage, on the other hand, works great to display favorite items and add some visual interest to the room. Whatever you choose, you want it to be easy for your child!

TOY STORAGE CUBES—Toy storage cubes are extremely popular for toy organization and can be used to store almost anything from games and puzzles to car and doll collections. Bigger playsets or boxed toys can just be placed directly into a cube, keeping a separate cube for each toy category, while toys with smaller parts can be placed into a labeled bin before being stored on the shelf. Some of the storage cubes also come with additional storage options such as drawers or slotted shelves to further divide the cube. Don't let stuff pile onto the top of the unit as this can make it look more cluttered.

TOY BINS—I like toy bins to store a large collection of something such as dress-up clothes or to hold all of the stuffed animals; however, smaller toys and toys that come with many accessories can easily get lost in the clutter making it difficult for kids to find what they want.

BASKETS—Baskets can be a nice way to provide some storage as well as a decorative element to the room. Limit each basket to one particular item or category of toys to make it easier to keep things organized. Baskets work well to store baby toys in one place, as well as blankets, books or stuffed animals and are easily portable for play.

CREATIVE STORAGE—Don't feel like you have to limit yourself to storage solutions specifically designed for toys, because any type of container or storage piece can work. Unused suitcases could hold dress-up clothes and be stored under the bed, storage boxes designed for nails or screws can hold smaller items such as art supplies or small drawer units designed for the home office could be used to sort building bricks. Take a look around your home first and see what you have before heading out to buy new organization products.

Step 4: Return Items and Evaluate

Place all of the toys back in their designated spots and go over any new changes with your children. While it may take some getting used to, stick with your system and get your children to assist with maintenance as much as possible.

After you have been using the system for a few weeks, spend a little time evaluating how it's working. If it's not staying as organized as you had planned, figure out what the problem might be. Is there a particular type of toy that's making the majority of the mess? Are your kids (or you!) not following the plan? Do you need to add another storage unit? Sometimes just a few tweaks here and there can make all of the difference. Whatever you do, don't give up! It may just take a little time and practice on everyone's part.

DIY Under the Bed Storage Tray

Utilizing the space under the bed is a great way to add some extra storage space for toys, out-of-season clothing or ongoing projects that the kids are still working on. You need to take into consideration the clearance space between the floor and the lower bed rails before deciding what you will actually be able to store here, so don't forget to look at this first. This project makes a two-foot-by-four-foot (61-by-122-cm) tray. If you would like a deeper storage unit, you could use 1 x 4 (19 by 101 mm) or 1 x 6 (19 by 152 mm) boards instead.

The corner brackets are more of a necessity for stability if you want higher sides on your tray. They are more for decorative purposes when using the 1 x 2 sides.

• •

Saw

1 x 2 boards, 12 feet (19 x 50 x 3,658 mm)

2 feet by 4 feet (61 x 122 cm) ½ inch (13 mm) A/C plywood

Nails or wood screws

Paint or stain

Lint-free rag (optional)

Corner braces with screws

Casters (optional)

Step 1: Cut the 1 x 2 Boards

Cut two 48-inch (122 cm) pieces and two 22½-inch (57-cm) pieces from the 1 x 2. If you have a miter saw, you can cut two 48-inch (122-cm) pieces and two 24-inch (61-cm) pieces, mitered at 45° across the ends. Sand all of the pieces smooth.

Step 2: Assemble the Unit

Line the 1 x 2s up along the edges of the plywood on the smooth side of the plywood. Drive nails or screws from the rough (underside) of the plywood into the 1 x 2s.

Step 3: Paint or Stain the Unit

If you are painting the tray, apply one coat of primer and two coats of paint followed by a light sanding with a fine-grit sandpaper. If you are staining, apply the stain as per the instructions on your stain and wipe off any excess with a lint-free rag. Allow to dry completely. We used a wood stain in walnut for our finish.

Step 4: Add the 'L' Brackets (Optional)

Spray paint the corner braces and screws if you choose. The braces can be added to the outside corners of the unit as a decorative element or applied to the inside of the corners if you don't want them as visible.

Step 5: Add the Casters (Optional)

If you have hardwood flooring in the bedroom, casters are definitely needed to avoid scratching the floor; however, for those of you with carpet, this is an optional step. Remember to take into account the height of the casters when you're looking at the clearance space available under the bed. Attach the casters using wood screws after pre-drilling the holes.

• •

DIY Industrial Shelves

These DIY Industrial Shelves are an inexpensive way to add some custom shelving to any space and can be used for a variety of storage and display needs. The measurements can easily be altered to allow you to pick the perfect-sized shelving for your space and just a few basic supplies are required. In addition to the kids' rooms, these can also be added to family rooms, bathrooms, dining rooms or any other area of your home that additional storage or display space is required.

The black steel pipe for this project can often be purchased at big-box home-supply stores; however, if the sizing that you would like is not available, plumbing stores will have more options. The number of units that you'll need depends on the length of the shelves and how heavy the objects will be that you will be placing on the shelf. The pipes come in a variety of lengths depending on the depth that you would like your shelves to be. We used 12-inch (31-cm) pipes for our shelf brackets. Since our shelf was 8 feet (244 cm) long, we went with three brackets per shelf, but this can be adjusted as needed.

I used a black spray paint with a hammered-metal finish. Clean the pipe with rubbing alcohol before painting, as it often is coated with oil. The cost of the board can vary greatly depending on the quality, type and thickness of the wood. Since we were painting ours and I wanted to keep it as inexpensive as possible, we used 1 x 12 pine board that was actually discounted due to some imperfections (19 x 305 mm). If you are staining, check to see that the finish on the wood is up to your expectations as you will see all of the imperfections much more.

Spray paint

¾-inch (20-mm) black or galvanized metal pipe

¾-inch (20-mm) pipe cap for each pipe

¾-inch (20-mm) floor flange for each pipe

Sanding block or palm sander

Two 1 x 12 by 8 foot boards (19 x 305 x 2,440 mm)

Paint or stain

Stud finder

Screws

Step 1: Spray Paint

Spray paint all of the piping pieces as well as the screws that you will be using with two coats of spray paint. To make it easier to spray the screws, stick them in a foam block to keep them upright.

Step 2: Prep the Boards

Sand down any rough spots on the boards. If you would like a more weathered look, round out the edges and corners with a palm sander until you achieve your desired effect. Wipe clean with a cloth.

(continued)

DIY Industrial Shelves (continued)

Step 3: Paint the Shelving

If you are painting the shelves, apply one coat of primer and two coats of paint followed by a light sanding with fine-grit sandpaper. If you are staining, apply the stain per the manufacturer's instructions and wipe off any excess with a lint-free rag. Allow to dry completely.

Step 4: Find the Studs and Mark Bracket Locations

Using a stud finder, mark where there are any studs are on the wall. Ideally you want to have your brackets mounted to a stud; however, depending on where you want to put the brackets and how long your board is, this may not work out to allow even spacing of the brackets. If you are attaching your shelving to drywall, you need to use anchors in those locations that the brackets can't be attached to the studs.

Step 5: Attach the Floor Flanges to the Wall

Attach the floor flanges using screws and anchors if needed. Once it's mounted you can screw in the pipe. Although there isn't technically a top and bottom to the flange, we did find that the pipe appeared most level if we had the flange aligned a certain way. Rotate your flange around if the piping does not appear level when you screw it into the flange.

Step 6: Add the Shelf

Lay the shelving over the pipe and screw on the pipe cap until it's snug against the shelving. We found that with the length and size of our shelving this was quite secure; however, if you would like to add further stability, you can purchase brackets to secure the pipe to the underside of the shelving.

Step 7: Add the Items

Add whatever items you would like to display or store on your shelves. To store smaller items, use bins or baskets to corral like items together and decrease some of the visual clutter. These shelving units work great for older children and teens and can also be used in spaces for younger children as a display unit or to hold items that you would like stored out of reach.

DIY Wooden Ledges and Sports Display

While I used these ledges to come up with a sports display for my son, they can also be used to display your child's story books in a reading nook, arrange photo frames in your family room or hold small storage items in your bathroom or kitchen. Just use your imagination! The size of the baseboard can also be increased from a 1 x 4 to a 1 x 6 if you would like to increase the depth of the shelf a little bit and, of course, the shelf can be customized to any length you choose. This is a super-simple DIY project, so don't be scared to give it a go. If you don't have a saw to cut down your wood pieces, you can generally get the wood cut down to size where you purchase it. For each shelf you need one piece of the 1 x 4 board and two pieces of the 1 x 2 board cut to the same length.

Saw

1 x 4 (19 x 89 mm) board cut to length (One per shelf)

1 x 2 (19 x 38 mm) board cut to the same length (You need two of these per shelf)

Sanding block

Nails or screws

Wood filler

Paint or stain

Cup hooks (optional)

Stud finder

Anchors (if unable to attach the shelf to a stud)

Step 1: Cut the Pieces to Length
Using a saw, cut the wood to the desired size. Sand down rough edges. You may also want to sand down the corners and edges for a more rustic look.

Step 2: Assemble the Pieces
Nail or screw (using pre-drilled holes) one of the 1 x 2 boards to the front of the 1 x 4 board keeping it flush with the bottom of the 1 x 4. The back 1 x 2 board will be screwed in from the bottom of the 1 x 4 so that it sits on top of the 1 x 4 instead of flush with the bottom.

Step 3: Apply Wood Filler
Use wood filler to fill in any nail or screw holes. Allow to dry and sand flat.

Step 4: Paint or Stain
Paint or stain your shelves with whatever color or finish you choose. If painting, apply one coat of primer first or use an all-in-one paint and primer.

Step 5: Add the Cup Hooks (Optional)
If you would like to have cup hooks on the bottom for hanging, measure the spacing and mark on the bottom of the board. Screw in the hooks.

(continued)

. . . .

Step 6: Hang the Shelves

The shelves are simply screwed into the wall through the back of the shelving unit. We used one screw on each end of the shelf for ours but you may need to add a third screw in the middle if you make a longer shelf. Whenever possible, attach the shelving unit to a stud. If this is not possible, mark out where you would like the hole to be and add anchors.

Step 7: Add Your Display or Storage Items

Have fun creating your display piece! For our shelves, we gathered up some sports medals, trophies and special mementos to create a fun sports display.

. . . .

Organize the Books

We have always loved to read with our kids and I feel that the easier books are to access, the more likely kids are to read them. Exposing children early to books can help instill a strong love of reading as they get older, and it's a lovely way to spend some quality time together. Keep books within easy reach for your child and set up a welcoming and organized book display so they can find what they're looking for.

Sort through and purge books at least a couple of times per year and determine what books are no longer being read so you can donate them. If you have a large selection of books, try keeping a smaller number of books in your child's room and rotate them around to avoid overwhelming your child with too many options. Purchase only those books that you know your child will love and treasure, or classics that you will likely read many times over.

When it comes to cutting down on clutter, making use of your public library is the best way to enjoy books while saving money. Second-hand stores are another way to get your child reading without accumulating large numbers of books that are never read again. Every time you head down to buy new ones, take a few of your old books to donate.

Books can be stored and displayed in a variety of ways including traditional book shelves, in bins and baskets, or on specific wall shelves designed to keep the books front facing. Depending on the space available and how many books you have, you may want to use a combination of these storage methods. Try the DIY Wooden Ledges (page 131) or these DIY Rain Gutter Bookshelves for easy, accessible book storage. (We used three for our shelves which were roughly 5 feet [152 cm] long.)

DIY Rain Gutter Bookshelves

I like kids' book storage that allows the books to face forward so that it's easy for little ones to see what they would like to read and easily pick out (and put away!) the books as needed. These bookshelves have lasted for many years in our son's room and have provided many hours of entertainment.

· ·

Hacksaw

Vinyl or metal rain gutters

Metal file

Stud finder

Gutter hangers

Drill and wood screws

Level

Gutter caps

Step 1: Determine the Shelf Length

Decide how many shelves you would like and how long you would like them to be. Use the hacksaw to cut down the gutters to length and file the rough ends smooth with a metal file. Note: If you do not have a hacksaw, most home improvement stores will cut these for you in-store, so have your measurements ready.

Step 2: Screw in the Gutter Hangers

Use the stud finder and mark out where the studs are on the wall. Ideally, you want to screw the gutter hangers into a stud; however, this may not always be possible if you want them to be evenly spaced along your shelf. If you can't drill into a stud, use wall anchors to add more support.

Mark how high you want the top of your bottom shelf to go and line up your gutter. Secure the gutter to the wall by screwing the gutter spacer into the stud or wall anchor. Use a level and mark where you need the other two screws to go and secure.

Step 3: Add Additional Shelves

Mark how far apart you want your shelves to be (you might want to try out some of your taller books on the first shelf to help you get an idea of how far you want them apart) and attach them in the same manner as the first shelf always checking to make sure they are level.

(continued)

· ·

DIY Rain Gutter Bookshelves (continued)

Step 4: Add Gutter Caps if Needed

Since our bookshelves are in a little nook, the ends are flush with the wall on both sides. If you have exposed ends, however, you will need to finish them off with gutter caps so there are no exposed metal edges. There is a right and left for these so be sure to purchase the correct amount of each.

Step 5: Add Finishing Touches

Add the books to the shelves, placing the bigger books in first and then filling in the spaces with smaller books. We also kept a few storage bins beneath the shelving to store extra books and would rotate some of these around to keep things fresh. Add some pillows, a quilt or a comfy beanbag chair for your child to cozy up in as she enjoys her space.

Organize the Homework/Art Station

Creating a homework area or art station doesn't have to be anything fancy or even require a lot of time or space. It's just a dedicated spot in your child's room (or whatever area of the house you choose) that provides a space for your child to work and create as well as a specific area for you to store all of the school and art supplies. The design of your station and the supplies required depends upon the ages, needs and interests of your children, but the basic setup will be the same.

Step 1: Choose the Location

Before picking a spot, take into consideration the space that's available in your home, the age of your children and the overall needs of your family. While setting it up in your child's room is ideal in terms of keeping the kids' items confined to one space, younger children may need a spot closer to you such as a section of your home office or a corner of the kitchen table. Some families like to set up one spot in the house for the whole family to use while others create an individual spot for each child.

Step 2: Choose the Style

An art station could be a desk, a portable cart or tote that you bring to the kitchen table, or even an art easel that is set up in a corner with some basic supplies. Think outside of the box if you are short on space; add a small fold-down table that could be mounted to a wall or convert an unused nook or alcove into a little creative retreat. Portable caddies, baskets or rolling carts can also be used to hold supplies and can then be easily stored away elsewhere.

Step 3: Organize the Supplies

Gather up all of your child's art and school supplies from wherever they may be around the house and bring them to your homework area. Sort them into categories such as pencils and pens, markers, pencil crayons or scissors, tossing any broken pieces and donating items that are no longer used. Recycle old papers, schoolwork and artwork unless they are special pieces that you will be keeping. Use canning jars, cups or caddies to corral similar supplies together.

If you have drawers in your desk area, divide larger drawers up into smaller units with inexpensive plastic bins or other drawer dividers. Label all drawers so each item has a specific spot to go.

Step 4: Set Up a Display Area

Almost all kids like to display their favorite works of art so, if space allows, set up an area that your kids can hang their creative work. Clipboards, corkboards or clothespins glued to a board hanging on the wall are all easy ways to display artwork that can be easily switched up. Purchase photo frames to show off your favorite pieces—there are even specific frames that open from the front to make switching up artwork a breeze. These could be placed on the DIY Wooden Ledges that were used for the sports display on page 133 or hung on the walls around your child's room.

Tips to Maintain a Healthy Weight in the Kids' Rooms

- Go through clothing items seasonally. If your kids are already starting to outgrow seasonal items, they will likely not fit them when the season returns the following year, so don't hold on to them if you don't have to.

- Involve your kids in the process. I feel that kids are more likely to follow the organization plan if they have had some input into how it's set up, and organizing is an important life skill. Teach children about decluttering early so they get used to the idea of letting items go when they no longer use them. Often children are quite motivated by knowing that their old items will be going to other children who will play with them. Older kids might like the idea of selling some of their items (with your assistance) and saving the money to buy something that they really want.

- Prepare for holidays. If you know your children will be getting a lot of new toys for holidays or birthdays, spend some time purging their old toys before the holiday arrives to make some room. Remember the "calories in and calories out" rule and get rid of as many items as you are bringing in.

- Use the library as much as possible to keep the book weight down. If there are any particular favorites that your child wants to read over and over again, you can always purchase those.

- Give your children experiences rather than material gifts for birthdays or holidays. A season pass to the zoo or science center, coupons for fun activities or a weekend away at one of their favorite destinations will create memories to last a lifetime.

CHAPTER 11

TAPERING OFF THE LAUNDRY ROOM

The laundry room can often be a challenge to organize depending on the size and location of your space. To make things even more difficult, there always seems to be a pile of laundry waiting to be done and a stack of clean clothes to be folded. Working with the space that you have and developing an efficient laundry system is essential to creating a functional space that works for the whole family.

While you may not have an actual room for your laundry space, you do want to make sure that you create a dedicated area that's specifically for your laundry equipment and supplies. If you have a basement laundry that is located in a general storage room, define your laundry area and don't allow random storage to invade this space. In order to keep the laundry organized, you need space to move around and do your thing, so storage boxes and other items just get in the way and clog up your system.

Shedding the Pounds

Unless your laundry space has been taken over by a lot of clutter from elsewhere in the house, it should be one of the quickest places to lose some pounds.

LAUNDRY CLEANING SUPPLIES—Go through all of your laundry products and toss any items that are old or no longer used. Check opened products to ensure that they have not reached their expiration dates. If you have multiple packages of the same product, combine them into one. Commit to using any open packages of supplies before starting new ones.

CLOTHES CLUTTER—If you are constantly dealing with piles of clothes in the laundry room, you need to come up with a new system of dealing with your laundry on a long-term basis (see page 144 for more information). For now, wash any dirty clothes, put away the clean clothes and get a little basket to hold random socks that do not have a pair. Make sure that you have a laundry basket or hamper in your laundry room to hold any incoming dirty clothes.

CLEANING SUPPLIES—If you have other household cleaning supplies in your laundry room, sort through all bottles and supplies and toss any empty bottles or items that you no longer use. Place supplies that need to be used first toward the front of the storage space.

HOUSEHOLD SUPPLIES—Sort through any household supplies that you have stored in the laundry room such as lightbulbs, paper towels or water filters. If you have anything that you haven't used in the past year, donate it or toss it. Store similar items together and have a dedicated spot for each item that you store.

CLEANING TOWELS—If you keep old towels for rags and cleaning jobs, sort through them and toss any that are getting torn or are extremely worn. Keep only the number of towels that you actually need and use. Donate any extras to an animal shelter.

MENDING SUPPLIES—Keeping your mending supplies close at hand for buttons that have fallen off or other quick touch-ups makes it easier to do these little tasks as they come up rather than have them pile up on you. Check through your kit and get rid of items that you don't need.

OTHER ITEMS—Return all items that you would like to keep but that don't belong in the laundry room to their proper location.

Building Strength: Exercises for the Laundry Room

In this section, we look at developing a strong organization system for both the laundry room space, as well as your overall laundry routine. This not only keeps your room more organized, but also makes the task of doing laundry much more efficient. Here are the exercises that we will be working on.

General Laundry Room Organization

Even though the laundry room is small, you can still think of setting it up in terms of functional zones. The basic zones of any laundry room include a storage area for laundry supplies, a zone with the appliances and a drying and folding area. Depending on your space, you may also have an ironing zone, a washing zone with a basin or sink or a storage zone for additional household products. Once you have an idea of how you want your space to function, you are ready to get started on the organization process itself.

Step 1: Empty Out the Space and Clean

Take everything out of the cabinets or shelving units in the laundry room and wipe them down. If you haven't cleaned under your washing machine and dryer in a while, you may want to move them out from the wall and vacuum the floor space.

As you empty out items, sort them into the keep, toss, donate and belongs elsewhere piles.

Step 2: Sort Your Keep Items

Make sure that all of your keep items belong in the laundry room and fit into one of the functional zones that you have decided on for this space. Group all of your keep items into similar categories. For example, you may choose to put all of your stain-removal products in one category, all of your laundry products for the washing machine in another category and all of your laundry products for the dryer in yet another category.

Step 3: Develop Your Storage Solutions

Assess your current level of storage and decide if it just needs a little reorganizing or if you need to come up with additional storage ideas. Here are some of the basic storage and space needs that you will likely have.

LAUNDRY SUPPLIES—You need a storage system to hold all of your basic laundry supplies such as detergent, dryer balls, laundry booster and stain removers. Cabinets are ideal to keep all of the cleaning supplies hidden out of sight, but shelving units (either wall mounted or free standing) are generally a much cheaper option. (Refer to the next section for more ideas on organizing your cabinets and shelves.) If there is no option for either of these, look for a rolling storage cart that can hold your basic supplies. Laundry supplies should only be stored on top of your washer and dryer as a last resort.

LAUNDRY HAMPER—To keep all of the incoming laundry under control, you should have a hamper or laundry basket close by the washing machine to hold items that are waiting for the laundry. If you have the space, you can even purchase multi-bin hampers so that your items can be pre-sorted into lights and darks.

FOLDING AREA—I find that the quicker I can fold my laundry after it's completed, the more likely it is to get done. Folding it right in the laundry room is the simplest way to do it, and there are usually minimal distractions to throw me off task. Folding can be done on a countertop, fold-down counter or directly on top of your washer or dryer. If you prefer to always fold your laundry while watching television or in another room, you may not need to make space for this.

IRONING BOARD AND SUPPLIES—I very rarely iron any of my clothing items so I don't keep an ironing board in our laundry room. If you do iron regularly, then having a space for the ironing board and iron may be more of a priority. Look for wall-mounted boards that can fold down when needed or hang the ironing board from hooks on the wall. Whatever type of ironing board you use, ensure that you can put it up and take it down easily so you aren't tempted to leave it up when it's not in use. A flat space always attracts clutter!

DRYING AREA—If you air-dry some of your clothing, you need an air-drying area. Items can be laid out flat on a towel on top of the washer and dryer if you just have an item or two, but this isn't really functional if you have a lot of items. Retractable clotheslines that mount to a wall are one of the easiest methods of adding some drying area and they take up very little space when not in use. Pull-out wall racks or expanding floor racks are other options.

Step 4: Add the Finishing Touches

Once all of your storage solutions are in place, put all of your keep items away in their specific locations. Use bins and baskets to keep like items together and make them easy to access from your cabinets or shelving. To make the space a little prettier, add a few decorative touches such as a photo frame or other artwork, a laundry room sign or a vintage washboard.

Organize the Laundry Cabinets or Shelving

If you don't have any cabinets or shelving in your laundry space, install some if possible or look for a free-standing cabinet or cubbies to store all of your supplies. Keep the top of your washing machine or counter space as free as possible to deal with the actual laundry. If you do want to keep some basic supplies on your counter space, corral them all into a tray, caddy or bin and keep them contained to the back third of the counter space.

You should have already decluttered your laundry items when you were working on your laundry room organization, so we are just going to look at some additional ideas for organizing the cabinets and shelving in this section. Sometimes it's the little things that can make a big difference in how your space functions, so try some of these simple ideas in your laundry room to help keep things more organized and running smoothly.

- Have a sock basket. Socks can easily get misplaced and separated when you're doing the laundry, so keep a basket handy to toss in any unmatched socks that you come across. Go through this once per month (or sooner if you are short on socks!) and match up as many socks as you can.

- Hang a list of common stain-removal strategies. Keep a list of how to get rid of common stains on the inside of your cabinet door and ensure that you are stocked with items needed for your most frequent stains.

- Have a collection spot for loose change. Mount a tray to the inside of your cupboard door or keep a small bowl or jar on the shelf to hold any treasures that you might find.

- Keep a wastebasket or lint collection container close to the dryer. Get in the habit of emptying out the lint tray in the dryer after every load and have a quick place that you can deposit the lint so it doesn't get left on the counter.

- Store laundry detergents and other products in glass jars to keep the look uniform. Laundry products can come in a variety of boxes and containers, so to keep the look uniform, consider storing them in alternative storage containers. Label anything that is not in its original packaging clearly and ensure that it's well out of the reach of younger children.

- Use bins and baskets to keep similar items together. Bins work well to hold smaller laundry items out of sight if you have open shelving and also make it much easier to access what you need from higher shelves. I use one bin for all of my stain-removal items and another bin for some extra laundry supplies. I also took an extra glass jar that I had left over from the kitchen and used it to store our wool dryer balls.

- Purchase shelving specifically designed for pipes. If you have awkward piping that is inhibiting you from using the storage space under your laundry room sink, look for storage shelves that can be adapted to fit around pipes.

Organize the Laundry System

If you feel like you can never get a good hold on your laundry, coming up with a plan that works for the needs of your family (and sticking to it!) can really put you back in control again. If you don't currently have a laundry routine in place, this might initially seem like a lot of work, but once it's integrated into your schedule, it makes things so much easier. Give it a valiant effort for a couple of months and see how it goes!

Step 1: Determine Laundry Hamper Location

Remember that the fewer hampers you have, the less running around you have to do when it comes to putting in a load of laundry. Bathrooms and bedroom closets tend to be the most popular place for storing laundry hampers as this is where the laundry tends to accumulate the most; however, if you have a multi-level house, you may want to keep a laundry hamper somewhere on each floor or by the washing machine. We have two hampers in our upstairs level—one in the bathroom for towels (as I prefer to wash these separately) and one in our master bedroom closet that is divided into darks and lights for all of the dirty clothing. This makes it much easier to know when a full load is ready to go instead of having to go around to individual laundry hampers in each bedroom. We also keep a laundry bin right in front of the washing machine for any incoming dirty laundry that originates on the main floor.

Step 2: Decide How You Want to Sort Your Laundry

Traditionally, laundry was always sorted into lights and darks with linens and delicates washed separately from other items. Personally, I still like to stick with this method, and wash each type of laundry a little bit differently, but I know lots of people who skip the sorting and just throw everything in together. If you are in the no-sort camp, I would still recommend doing a separate load for particularly dirty clothes or new clothes that may bleed. Washing microfiber and certain sportswear (such as yoga pants) with fluffy towels or other high-lint-producing items is also not a good mix. If you do sort your laundry, look for laundry hampers that have dividers so you can sort your laundry as you place the dirty items in. It doesn't take any extra time and everything is ready to go when needed. For those of you who choose to have a separate hamper in each bedroom, it might be easier to sort your laundry by person rather than by lights and darks.

Step 3: Determine How Other Family Members Will Contribute

How you divide up the task of doing laundry is based on a number of factors, including the number of family members you have, the ages of your children or how much laundry you tend to produce. If you have older children, you may decide to make them responsible for doing their own laundry while other families like to stick with one main person doing the laundry. In either case, it's important that your family members know what is expected of them. Even if they are not doing the actual laundry, kids can still contribute to the process in a number of ways such as dividing their clothing up into lights and darks when they put it in the hamper, making sure that their clothing is not bunched up and putting their own clothing away.

Step 4: Choose a Regular Washing Routine

There are a few ways that you can set up a regular washing routine. Choose what works best for your schedule and what seems the easiest for you to follow through with. Make sure that your family knows when you are and are not going to be doing laundry.

DAILY ROUTINE—Each day, do one complete load of laundry from start to finish. This is the routine that we use, and I find that it's pretty easy to stick with and just becomes part of my regular daily schedule. If you miss a day, it's no big deal. It also makes it pretty much impossible to run out of the basic necessities as I can just decide in the morning what items take priority for washing. I like to get the laundry in first thing in the morning so it's out of the way and then switch it to the dryer as soon as possible. I can then pick whatever time works best to fold it and have it ready for the kids to put away when they tidy their rooms before bed.

LAUNDRY DAY ROUTINE—If you just want to get your laundry done in one big go, you may prefer designating one day of the week as your laundry day and getting through all of your laundry at once. If you have quite a bit of laundry to do, it requires you to be home for a large part of the day, but on the positive side, it's just one day of the week and then you don't have to think about it again. Put away the clean laundry as you go or you will be stuck with a big batch of laundry to fold at the end of the day!

SPECIFIC ITEMS ON CERTAIN DAYS—If you divide your laundry up, you may wish to do certain items on specific days. For example Saturday mornings may be when you always wash the bed linens and the clothing is always done Sunday nights.

THE RANDOM ROUTINE—Specific routines are not for everyone and some people just prefer to do their laundry as they need it. Just be sure not to let things pile up for too long, as it can start to get overwhelming after a while.

Step 5: Make Putting Things Away as Easy as Possible

The folding and putting things away is often where people get stuck when it comes to doing laundry. The more laundry you have piled up, the more overwhelming it becomes and the more effort it takes to complete it. In addition, items can become wrinkled if left in a pile for too long, requiring you to take more time and energy to iron them. The easier things are to put away, the more likely you (and your family) will be to actually do them, so think of strategies to simplify this stage.

BINS—For kids' clothing that you don't need to worry about wrinkles, like socks, underwear, pajamas, etc., have these items stored in bins at kid-level so they can just be tossed in there. It makes it super easy for the kids to put them away and easy for them to access.

HANGERS—If you have the space, store clothes as much as possible on hangers. You don't have to take the time to fold them, it makes everything easy to see and it keeps them wrinkle-free. Kids and folding clothes neatly in drawers just don't go together.

Tips to Maintain a Healthy Weight in the Laundry Room

- Sort through the random-sock basket monthly and pair up socks. Toss any socks with holes or ones that you have not been able to find a mate for.

- Quickly check through your cabinets and shelving every month, to make sure that everything is in its proper location.

- Purchase clothing that's easy to launder so you don't have to worry about special washing instructions

- Get in the habit of folding and putting away clean clothes as soon as possible when the load is finished. Don't start a load of laundry that you won't have time to complete.

CHAPTER 12

TRIMMING DOWN THE OUTDOOR SPACES

The outdoor spaces are often forgotten when you're organizing your home, but it's the first thing that everyone else will notice. Organizing your outdoor areas not only boosts your curb appeal, it can also increase your living space during the milder months and provide you with your own personal oasis to relax in.

Obviously the best time of the year to work on your yard is when the weather is mild but you're not yet into the extreme heat of the summer. Depending on where you live, you may be able to get out in the yard even before spring hits while others may need to wait until later in the season. Choose whatever month works best for you, but remember that the earlier in the season you can get it done, the more time you will have to enjoy it!

Shedding the Pounds

Tackling your outdoor spaces can often be an overwhelming task, especially if you live in colder climates where the yard can take a beating throughout the winter months. You just need to approach it the same way you would with any of your indoor spaces and take things one area at a time. Sometimes your excess weight may be in the form of overgrown weeds or shrubs rather than actual objects that you have purchased, but it will all still be dealt with in the same manner.

OUTDOOR TOYS—Examine all toys that have been left outdoors and toss anything that is damaged or broken. Evaluate the remaining toys and donate any that your children no longer use or play with. Test any blow-up toys to ensure that they are still holding their air.

PATIO FURNITURE—Inspect all patio furniture and determine what you still use and what needs to be tossed or donated. Many of these can look quite old and worn but just require a good cleaning to restore them back to their glory days.

OUTDOOR ACCESSORIES AND DECOR ITEMS—Check these for significant signs of wear and tear or sun damage and assess if they're still adding beauty to your space. Toss old items and donate items in decent condition that are no longer your taste.

WEEDS—Pull out any weeds and place in yard waste.

PLANTS, TREES AND BUSHES—Pull out any greenery that is dead. Trim back your current plants, trees and shrubs so they look neat and tidy. Depending on what plants and trees you have, trimming is only recommended at certain times of the year (generally spring and early fall) so consult with an arborist if you are unsure of when and how your particular varieties of plants and trees should be pruned.

DEBRIS—Gather up any debris or garbage that may be taking away from the beauty of your yard and garden spaces.

PLANTERS—Assess what planters you still want to use and donate or toss the rest. Pull out any dead items that are left over from the previous year and place them in yard waste. Plastic planters can be refreshed with a new coat of spray paint if the paint is chipped and flaking.

OTHER ITEMS—Return all items that you would like to keep but don't belong outdoors to wherever they belong. Put them away immediately.

Building Strength: Exercises for Your Outdoor Spaces

Give your outdoor spaces the same time and consideration as you do to your indoor spaces. By developing some strong organization systems and taking the time to define your functional zones, you will be able to create a healthy outdoor living area that your whole family can use and enjoy.

Organize the Yard Space

The first thing that you need to do when it comes to organizing your yard is to determine what your goals are for the finished space. Do you just want a tidy, low maintenance yard or are you an avid gardener who would like a vegetable garden and flower beds? Will you be using your yard for a lot of entertaining or do you just prefer a quiet retreat? Once you have decided on this, you should be ready to get to work.

Step 1: Start with a Clean Slate

There is nothing that will have as much impact on your outdoor spaces as a good thorough cleaning. Once you have removed the excess weight and have trimmed everything down as much as possible (see Shedding the Pounds on the previous page), give your driveway, walkways and cement patios a good sweeping and/or power washing (if not in a drought-affected area). If you don't own a power washer, see if you can borrow one from a friend or rent one from a home-building store. Use a hose and wood cleaner to wash any wooden decks or porches.

Step 2: Organize Your Yard into Zones

Just like you would organize a room into functional zones, you'll need to organize your yard into functional areas. You may wish to include a garden area, a fire pit zone, a specific place for lounging, a play area for the kids or a potting zone or outdoor shed. You may also need an area for your garbage bins, recycling or outdoor waste. Dividing the yard up into zones makes your space look less cluttered, clearly defines where all of your items should go (and stay), and allows you to make the most out of your outdoor space. Remember that the more zones you have, the more work required to maintain them, so only create what you have the time, energy and desire to keep up with. If you spend all of your time creating the areas but don't have the time to enjoy them, they will just be added weight that will hold you down.

Step 3: Choose Your Storage Solutions and Design Plan

What storage, if any, you will need for your yard is really dependent on what zones you have chosen to set up.

GARDEN SUPPLIES—If you are an avid gardener and like to keep your supplies out in your yard, look for a weather-resistant storage unit that can hold all of your supplies. There are fold-up units available that can be quite space efficient or you may wish to purchase a small garden shed or covered potting table. If you don't require a lot of equipment or can store the majority of it in the garage, a storage tote or caddy may be all you need. Whatever you decide, choose a specific location where you will keep these items and ensure that they are protected from the weather.

KIDS' AREA—Even though your kids will likely use the whole yard, try to contain their toys to one section for storage purposes. An outdoor storage box works well to corral all of their toys, keeping the grass clutter-free and protecting the toys from the elements when not in use. If you have a playhouse in your yard, you could use a large plastic bin to hold the toys instead and keep this in or beside the house. For those of you with a sandbox, having a top not only keeps out the neighborhood cats, but can also keep all of the sand toys out of sight when not in use.

LOUNGE AREA—If you don't have a back patio or deck, you may want to use another area of your yard for a lounge space or picnic area. If you live in an area that can receive a lot of rain or you'd like some added shelter from the sun, consider setting up a gazebo to define your space. This helps to protect any patio cushions or other items that can be damaged from the rain (or sun) and eliminates the need for you to haul your pillows in and out of your space due to the weather. Purchase only items that you will be able to store properly over the winter months. When choosing accessories, look for items that are both decorative and functional such as pretty outdoor lanterns that provide some nighttime lighting, candles to keep away the bugs or a patio side table that could double as extra seating.

Step 4: Finishing Touches

If you choose, you may want to add some finishing touches to your yard with flowers, planters or other decorative items. Remember that it's much better to have less and maintain it properly than to have too much and not have the time to take care of it and enjoy it. Keep a healthy balance between your yard's weight and the amount of time that you can (and want!) to put into it. You will then have much more time to relax and actually use the space that you have created.

DIY Yard Waste Storage

If you store garbage, recycling or yard waste bins in your yard, these areas can often be an eyesore and can quickly become cluttered. This DIY Yard Waste Storage contains everything in one area and hides the ugly bins. While ours was designed to hold five rubber garbage bins, you can always tailor the measurements down to better fit your needs. I also opted to leave a cover off the top to make it easier to just dump things in from above, but you could easily cover it if you prefer, as there is access from the front.

I have given the approximate measurements for all of our boards but this can be adjusted as needed depending on the size that you would like to make your unit. I recommend that you cut the pieces as you go so you can make small adjustments to the measurements as needed. We used two posts on each end as well as two posts in the middle of the unit. If you make a smaller unit, you may not need the two posts in the middle. We cut our boards to the following measurements:

These directions are to make an enclosure that measures 10 feet long by 26 inches deep by 3 feet high (305 x 66 x 91 cm) and easily holds five garbage bins.

• •

Miter saw

Three 6-foot 4 x 4 (89 x 89 x 1829 mm) posts

Five 10-foot 2 x 4 (38 x 89 x 3048 mm) boards

Outdoor paint and primer

Six 4 ft x 8 ft lattice sheets

Spray painter (optional)

Spray Paint

3-inch (7.5-cm) deck screws

Metal square

Five 8-foot 2 x 2 (38 x 38 x 2438 mm) boards

Jigsaw or circular saw

Nails

Hinges (8)

Gate hooks (2 sets)

Step 1: Cut the Posts, Tops and Bottoms

Cut the 4 x 4 posts in half to make six 36-inch (91-cm) posts. Cut four 120-inch (305-cm) lengths of 2 x 4, mitering at 45° across the face. Cut four 26-inch (66-cm) lengths of 2 x 4, mitering at 45° across the face.

Step 2: Paint or Stain the Wood

You can either paint the wood prior to assembly or assemble the whole unit and then paint it. I did a little bit of both but found it easier to have the wood pre-painted and then just do some touch-ups after it was completed. For the lattice, I highly recommend using a paint sprayer if available, as it will significantly cut down on your time for all of the little crevices.

(continued)

• •

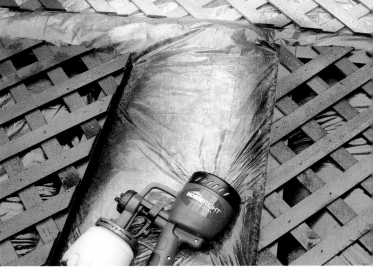

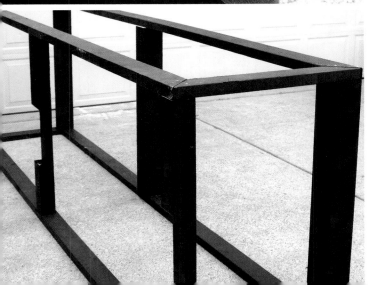

DIY Yard Waste Storage (continued)

Step 3: Build the Front and Back of the Frame

Screw the long 2 x 4s flat onto the ends of the 4 x 4 posts, ensuring that everything is square to make the front of the frame. Repeat to make the back of the frame.

NOTE: We used a metal square frequently throughout this project to ensure that everything we were constructing was square.

Step 4: Connect the Front and Back of the Frame

Stand up the posts and screw the cross pieces in. Flip the unit over (you will need a couple of people for this) and do the same thing on the bottom.

NOTE: We customized the back posts on our unit (instead of using the 4 x 4 posts) to fit flush against the angle on our house. Because this is unique to our home, I did not include this in the tutorial.

We put the unit in place at this point so it would not be as heavy to move, but you can complete the full project before moving it if desired.

Step 5: Build the End Inserts

Cut the 2 x 2s to form a frame that will fit into the ends of the unit (ours measured 19 x 33 inches [48 x 84 cm]). Nail the lattice down onto the back of the frame to stabilize all of the pieces and use a jigsaw or circular saw to cut the lattice down to size.

Once the inserts are completed, screw them into the posts, pre-drilling the holes if needed.

(continued)

Step 6: Build the Door Frames

The door frames are constructed the same way as the end inserts although your frame measurements will be different. Our door frames measure approximately 27 inches by 33 inches (69 x 84 cm). Make the door width approximately an inch (6 mm) less than the opening to allow for the doors to open and close properly.

Step 7: Spray-Paint Hinges (Optional)

You don't have to do this step, but I chose to spray-paint the hinges and screws in an oil-rubbed bronze so they would blend in more with the paint on the wood. To paint the screws, stick them in a foam block so you can easily spray them all at once.

Step 8: Attach the Doors

Once the hinges have dried, attach the doors to the frame and add the gate hooks.

Step 9: Finishing Touches

Touch up any areas that need paint. I didn't fill in the screw holes with wood putty since the unit will just be outdoors, but you could do this if you choose. To prevent the bottom from getting muddy, lay down some landscape fabric (to keep weeds from growing through) and top with crushed limestone or other rock. Add your garbage cans.

Organize the Outdoor Entryway

Whether you have a front porch, veranda, patio or just a simple walkway to the door, taking a little time to make your outdoor entryway a warm and inviting space will go a long way in increasing your curb appeal and will make your home much more welcoming for your guests. It really doesn't take much—just a few little touches can make all the difference!

Step 1: Remove Everything from the Porch

Take everything off your front porch and give the porch a good cleaning with a hose, wood cleaner or power washer depending on what it's made of. If it needs repainting or staining, you can do it now if you have the time or put it on your to-do list for the near future.

Step 2: Sort Items

Evaluate everything that you have and pick out only what you still love. Throw any dead plants into yard waste and toss items that are severely weathered or damaged. If you have any decorative items that are still in good shape but are not really your style anymore, donate them.

Step 3: Add Function and Personality

There are likely a few functional items that you need to have in your front entry as well as some items that you may choose to have to increase your curb appeal. Start with those items that you need and add in some decorative elements.

MAILBOX—Some homes are required to have a mailbox of some sort, either at the end of the driveway or by the front of the house, while others use community mailboxes. If you do have a mailbox at your home, choose one that suits your style as well as the exterior of the house. If yours is getting worn touch it up with some paint or replace it if needed.

HOUSE ADDRESS—Your house numbers should be as visible as possible. Make sure you don't have any overgrown bushes that are covering them up. We learned the hard way that the postal service will not deliver packages to your home if the house numbers are not clearly readable! Combine function with design and look for pretty ways to display your house address—from easy DIY projects to store-bought versions, there is something for every style.

OUTDOOR STORAGE—Decide what items (if any) you would like to have on your front porch. If you are short on space on the inside, and you have a covered porch, you could use this area for some additional storage if needed. A shoe tray, for example, could be used for boots or other wet shoes (see DIY Pebble Shoe Tray page 172), or you could look for an outdoor bench or decorative storage unit for inexpensive items such as kids' toys or a pet leash and pet toys.

DOORMAT—A front doormat is a great way to dress up the space while still providing a valuable function. Choose something that represents your style and personality. If you don't have storage for extra mats, find one that is non-seasonal so it can remain out year round.

PLANTS AND FLOWERS—Plants and flowers are a wonderful way to add color and character to your entry; however, make sure you pick only what you have the time and energy to keep up with. Having no plants at all is better than having unkempt planters that are overgrown or dying. Even one or two can change the look of the space so don't go overboard!

DECORATIVE ITEMS—Choosing a couple of decorative items for the front porch can really help to dress up your space. If you want something low maintenance, choose one or two items that can be displayed all year round so you don't have to remember to change them up each season. If you like adding seasonal touches, switch up a door wreath or seasonal sign.

Organize the Back Patio or Deck

If you are lucky enough to have a back patio or deck space for outdoor living and entertaining, just think of it as an extension of your indoor spaces when you are coming up with your design plan. Use area rugs, comfortable furniture, end tables, lighting and decorative items just like you would if you were designing a family room—just make sure they are all weather-proof for your climate!

Step 1: Empty Out the Space

You should have already done a good cleaning of your back patio when you were organizing the yard in general, so now it's just about refining the space to make it more functional and enjoyable. Clearing everything off of the patio allows you to start fresh in creating your vision of your perfect backyard retreat.

Step 2: Define the Zones

Before you start the actual design process, take a few minutes to visualize what you would like to use the space for and how you want it organized. Do you envision yourself eating outside on a regular basis? Are you looking to create more of a quiet retreat or a place to read a book? Or do you want a great entertainment space to enjoy with your friends and family? Maybe it's even all of the above. Write down everything that you would like to use your space for and use that as a springboard for your patio design. If not everything fits on the patio itself, consider creating other rooms elsewhere in your backyard if you have the space.

Zones on your patio could include an eating area, a beverage bar, a BBQ area, a lounging area, a sitting or reading area based on what you want and will actually use. Pick your priorities and work with those zones first. You can always add more later if you find that you still have the space and a need.

Step 3: Anchor the Space with an Area Rug

Just like my indoor spaces, I find that starting with a great area rug is a good place to start when designing and defining a room. Choose a color and pattern that you like that you can build on with the rest of your design and decor.

Step 4: Add Your Furniture Back In

Keeping the function of the space in mind, add furniture where it makes the most sense and determine what pieces you may not need. For example, maybe your vision for your patio is an outdoor lounge area but your large patio table is weighing down the space even though you never eat at it. There are no rules for what your space has to contain—just make sure that every item serves a purpose and is actually used. Start by putting in the bigger pieces of furniture that are must-haves for you and then add in the smaller pieces and other items as space allows.

When it comes to purchasing new items for your patio, don't feel that you have to purchase a huge coordinating patio set all at once. You can mix and match items of various materials to add more interest and buy things as your budget allows. By always keeping your organization plan in mind, you can avoid buying pieces that you won't use or that won't fit into your space. If you are tight on space, look for multi-functional pieces such as a table that can be used as storage or a bench for seating if needed.

The other aspect to consider when it comes to your furniture and other items on your patio is long-term storage. Especially if you live in a colder climate, your furniture needs to be winterized, and less weather-resistant pieces, cushions, small decorative accessories, etc. need to be stored out of the elements for the winter months to avoid being damaged. Make sure you have a plan for all of this when you are deciding what to keep and what to give away as well as when you are purchasing new items.

Step 5: Finishing Touches

Once you have all of the main items in your space, it's time for all of the details. When thinking of decor items, use items that are pretty and add personality while still providing a useful function. Use patio umbrellas, pergolas, arbors, trellises or shrubs to provide at least a little shady space on your patio to get out of the sun. Colorful cushions are a great way to add comfort as well as a nice pop of color to your outdoor space. Make sure you're using cushions with an outdoor fabric to resist the sun's rays and offer some water resistance, and ensure that you have available storage for them during periods of bad weather and over the winter months. Patio string lights or solar lanterns look beautiful at night and can allow you to enjoy your outdoor area even longer.

DIY BBQ Organizer

If you use your grill often, it's handy to have one spot to organize and store your supplies so you don't have to constantly run in and out of the house. A rolling caddy is one option that would work if you have the room, but this simple wall-mounted DIY BBQ Organizer does the trick nicely and takes up minimal space. Depending on the space and amount of items that you want to store, choose the dimensions that you would like your organizer to be. These directions are for an organizer about 31 inches x 36 inches (78 cm x 92 cm). If you are not comfortable using a saw you could have your wood cut down at the home-building store where you purchase your wood. While they will sometimes do this for free, there may be a small fee associated with this. The project can be made with butt joints instead of miter joints, but that changes the cutting measurements for the vertical frame pieces to 1½ inches (3.7 cm) less.

Miter saw (or handsaw and miter box)

7 pieces 1 x 2 by 6 feet (19 x 38 x 1828 mm) pine boards

Sandpaper

Exterior paint or stain

Nails or wood screws

Four metal flat corner L braces

Over the door hooks and/or baskets, S hooks, cup hooks or other storage items

Wood filler

Step 1: Cut the Pieces for the Outer Frame

Using a miter saw, cut two 1 x 2 boards to 31 inches (78 cm) and two 1 x 2 to 36 inches (92 cm). Miter the ends to form a 45 degree angle for the corners of your frame. The pieces will be standing upright on the narrow side.

Step 2: Cut the Pieces for the Inner Frame

Measure the width and length of the inside of the outer frame and cut four 1 x 2 pieces to form the inner frame. Ours measured 29.5 inches (75 cm) and 34.5 inches (88 cm). Miter the corners across the board face. These pieces will lay flat on the inner border of your outer frame.

Step 3: Cut the Cross Pieces to Fit Inside the Outer Frame

Cut three horizontal cross pieces and two vertical cross pieces to fit. These should be the same measurements as your inner frame pieces; however, do not miter the edges.

(continued)

Step 4: Paint or Stain Your Pieces

Sand down your pieces and apply the paint or stain as desired. Be sure to use an outdoor paint or stain for this process to make your project more weather resistant. If you choose, you could just paint it all after it's completely put together (this may be easier if you are spray-painting or using stain); however, when painting with a brush, I find that it's easier to paint first and then just do minor touch-ups if needed after it's all put together.

Step 5: Assemble All of the Pieces Together

Nail the inner frame and outer frame pieces together on each side. Remember that the inner frame pieces should lay flat while the outer pieces lay upright.

Using a flat L bracket on the back of the frame, join the four pieces of the frame together with wood screws. Pre-drill holes to avoid splitting whenever using screws.

Mark where you want the width pieces to go so they are evenly spaced. Screw in the width pieces from the back side of the frame.

Flip the frame over and mark where you want the length pieces to go so they are evenly spaced. Screw these from the back into the width pieces.

Add frame hooks to the top sides of the organizer. Hang from wood studs or use anchors to secure to wall.

Step 6: Fill in Corner Gaps if Needed and Retouch Paint

If you have any gaps in the corner joints, fill with wood filler. Allow to dry and paint. Touch up any paint as needed to the rest of the organizer.

Step 7: Finishing Touches

Add whatever accessories you would like to fit your needs. You can use S hooks to hang BBQ tools or oven mitts or look for over the door hanging hooks or storage units to store jars or other supplies. Add a cup hook on the side to hang an apron. In addition to BBQ supplies, you could also use the organizer to display flowers or hold party supplies such as napkins, straws and cups.

Tips to Maintain a Healthy Outdoor Weight

- Get in the habit of storing outdoor items such as toys, backyard games or garden supplies away immediately when not in use. Not only will this make your yard appear much tidier, but it also protects your items from the elements and allows them to last longer.

- Develop a regular maintenance plan for any garden beds, planters, trees and shrubs to keep them healthy-looking and prevent them from becoming overgrown.

- Have a storage plan for all outdoor items that need to be stored away during times of inclement weather.

CHAPTER 13

CUTTING BACK THE MUDROOM AND ENTRYWAYS

· ·

The entryway is the first place you land when you enter your home, and it can be a huge source of clutter. By really evaluating your storage needs, cutting down on unneeded accessories and making all of those items that you use on a daily basis easily accessible, you can create a pretty space that is welcoming to come home to.

Your design and organization plan will likely differ slightly depending on whether you have a separate entry or mudroom for just family members or if you only have one main entrance that is used for both family and visitors; however, you ideally want to keep the entryways reserved for just your main day-to-day items that come and go from your home, and not for long-term storage.

· ·

Shedding the Pounds

To keep your entryways functional and welcoming, you need to get rid of any excess weight that is clogging it up. Since this is the first point of entry into the house, it's often an area that collects a lot of items that really belong elsewhere in the house. Your entryways should just contain those items that you use regularly, so get rid of that extra weight!

OUTERWEAR—Go through all of your coats and donate those items that no longer fit or are no longer your style. Try them on in front of a mirror to see how they really look. If you're short on space, put out-of-season coats in storage or another closet space.

FOOTWEAR—Keep only shoes that are comfortable and fit you well. There's no point in keeping that pretty pair of heels that just gives you blisters every time you put them on. Consider storing out-of-season shoes or those your wear less frequently elsewhere, especially if you have a small mudroom or entryway.

OUTDOOR ACCESSORIES—Check that all gloves and mittens are a pair and assess what you actually need and wear. Toss any items with holes. If you have a lot of a particular item, choose your favorites and donate the rest. Again, consider storing off-season items elsewhere if you are short on space.

PURSES AND BAGS—Keep only what you use and love. Limit storage in the entryway to seasonal items only and those that are used on a regular basis.

KEYS—Sort through all of your keys and ensure that you know what each of them is for. Label them as you go. Toss old keys that you no longer use.

SUNGLASSES—Toss any broken sunglasses or extras that you don't need.

LOOSE CHANGE—Gather up any loose change as you go and keep a little bowl or jar for this somewhere in your entryway.

PAPERWORK, NEWSPAPERS, MAIL, ETC.—Go through any loose papers, receipts, etc. that may be in your entryways. Toss or recycle those items that are no longer needed and put the rest away where they belong. Get in the habit of taking all paperwork directly to your family command center (or other short-term paper storage that you created) instead of dumping it as soon as you come in the door.

SCHOOL GEAR—If your kids store their school backpacks and other school items in the front entry, sort through backpacks and clear out any junk. Keep all school-related items stored in the backpack.

OTHER ITEMS—Return all items that you would like to keep but don't belong in the entryways to wherever they belong. Put them away immediately.

Building Strength: Exercises for the Mudroom and Entryways

Depending on the layout and size of your home, the amount of storage space in your entryways can vary greatly. The key point to remember is that the amount of stuff you have in the entry needs to fit the space! Once you have cut back on your items as much as possible, you need to come up with an organization plan to support the weight that you have left or come up with an alternative storage space.

Design Your Entryway Organization Plan

Your entryway will be much more functional if you take some time to think about your goals for the space and how you envision the space working in your home. Like any other area that you organize, you need to maximize the space that you have and create a simple storage plan for all of your items that will be stored there. If you have multiple entry spots in your home (such as a mudroom off the garage as well as a front entry that you use), follow these steps with each space.

Step 1: Clear Everything Out of the Space

Remove everything from the entryway, sorting items into keep, toss, donate and belongs elsewhere piles. Be honest about what you actually use and what you really need to keep—we often have many more items here (especially coats and shoes!) than we actually use.

Step 2: Decide What Will Be Kept in the Space

Keeping in mind the space that you have available and any alternative storage spaces that you could use, decide what items you need to keep in your entryway in order to make it functional for your family and what items you could store elsewhere. Remember that entryways should be reserved primarily for items that regularly leave and come back into the house. This can include shoes and coats that are worn on a daily basis, one or two purses, in-season outdoor accessories that you use, such as sunglasses or scarves or items that you use regularly to take your pet outside. If you have a smaller entryway or not a lot of closed storage, it's best to store out-of-season items in a storage space, hung in an extra closet or contained in space-saver bags. This also gives you a chance each season to reevaluate what you have used and what you haven't and may help you avoid packing on some excess weight in the future.

Step 3: Choose Storage Solutions

Coming up with a stylish and functional entryway plan can involve a little bit of planning and creative thinking. Coats and shoes are most likely the items that are taking up the most amount of space in your entryways, so they're a good place to start when it comes to organizing this area. Once you have tossed or donated those items that you no longer use and eliminated excessive items, it's time to come up with an organization system for those items that are left.

OUTERWEAR—Coats and jackets need to have a designated place to hang in the entryway whether it's on coat hooks that are mounted to the wall, a coat closet, or other free-standing options such as a coat tree. A mix of both open and closed storage solutions is generally ideal and provides a good balance between maintaining easy access and containing the clutter. Coat hooks and open storage tend to be easier for kids to use while closed storage works best for bulkier items and items that are used a little less frequently. Make sure that each person in your household has their own area or hook to hang their coats. Have a set number of coats that each person is allowed to have in this area depending on the space that you have available and stick with this plan. Extra coats or hoodies that are in-season can be stored in bedrooms and rotated out if there isn't enough space in the entryway.

SHOES AND OTHER FOOTWEAR—Shoes can pile up quickly, and if your plan is to take your shoes off at the front door (or other entry point), you need to provide enough shoe storage in this area to accommodate them all. Have a specific number of shoes that each family member is allowed to keep at the entryway and rotate shoes seasonally or as needed. If possible, store larger winter boots and rain boots on a shoe tray on the front porch or in the garage (see page 172 for a DIY Pebble Shoe Tray option).

If you have a small entryway, tall shoe cabinets are a great way to go to maximize your vertical space. The IKEA unit in our front entry holds 18 pairs of adult shoes (and more if they are kid-sized) and also provides some additional storage space on top to hold a basket for keys, spare change, sunglasses, etc. Pretty bins and baskets are another easy way to contain your shoes and can be stored in storage cubes. Use a different bin for each family member or one larger basket for all of the kids' shoes. While this isn't quite as organized, it is simple and will increase the likelihood of getting those shoes off the floor and contained in one designated spot.

ACCESSORIES—Accessories should all have a specific place to be stored. You can sort these by type or by family member. Storage bins and baskets tend to be the easiest way to keep all of these items contained and could be stored in a closet, storage cube or under a bench.

SEATING—If you have room, it's nice to have a bench or other seating available for taking shoes on and off. To optimize its function, look for a bench with built-in storage underneath the seat or one with space underneath it for a shoe tray or extra storage bins. A small chair in the corner can also work if you're short on space.

Step 4: Put It All Together

Start adding your items back into the space making sure that everything has a dedicated home. If you have some space available, add a couple of welcoming touches such as a flower vase, photo frames or a decorative pillow for seating. See the section on how to organize the drop zone on page 175 for ideas on how to organize all of your smaller items such as keys, sunglasses, wallets, etc.

DIY Pebble Shoe Tray

Pebble shoe trays are a pretty way to store your most frequently used shoes or to keep for guests' shoes when they are visiting. I have two versions that I use—a plastic tray for winter boots and other wet or really dirty shoes that can easily be hosed down, and a wooden tray that is used more for guests and dressier shoes.

Wooden or plastic tray

Casters and wood screws (optional)

River rocks or other pebbles

Glue (optional)

Step 1: Add Casters (Optional)

If you are going to be storing your tray under a bench or just want to have it more portable, adding casters makes it much easier to access your shoes, as you can easily slide it in and out without worrying about damaging the floor. I have unidirectional casters on our tray under our bench so it just rolls forward and back, but you can also choose to purchase multidirectional casters if you will be moving it around more. Simply attach the casters with wood screws to the base of your unit. Drill pilot holes to prevent the wood from splitting.

Step 2: Design the Layout

Spread out the rocks and decide on the general layout. Some of the river rock packages can come with bigger rocks than others so just disperse the bigger rocks evenly around the tray and fill in the gaps with the smaller pebbles.

Step 3: Secure Rocks in Place (Optional)

If you are concerned about little ones playing with the rocks or if you want to easily hose things down, you can glue the pebbles down using a waterproof multipurpose glue. For our trays, the rocks on the plastic tray are glued down while the rocks on our wooden tray are just loose. I can still use a narrow vacuum attachment on the wooden tray to vacuum up any loose debris without disturbing the rock layout.

Step 4: Add Shoes

One of the benefits of the smaller, plastic trays is that they can easily be moved around to wherever you need them. Use them on a covered porch or in the garage to allow wet shoes to dry or move them between entryways as needed for extra storage.

Organize the Entryway Closet

While an entryway closet would ideally be located right at the entry and be kept exclusively for entryway items, you have to use what you've got. So, if you don't have the perfect entryway closet, look around the house to see what else you could use. Our entryway closet is slightly off the entry down the main hallway and also functions as storage for our cleaning supplies. By optimizing the use of space and designating a specific spot for each item, it still functions well and provides enough storage to fit all of our needs. The tips given in this closet design are the same steps that I go through with every closet space, so don't limit this plan to just the entryway.

Step 1: Empty and Clean
Empty out the closet space and sort items into keep, toss, donate and belongs elsewhere. Give the closet a thorough cleaning especially into the corners. Wipe down the walls if needed.

Step 2: Group the Items into Categories
Once you have gotten rid of all of the items that you no longer need or use, separate them into similar categories. For this closet we have coats, shoes, keys and accessories as well as brooms/mops, cleaning supplies and smaller equipment.

Step 3: Plan Out the Design
Once you know how much space you'll need for each category, you can work out your storage plan. I find that it's easier to start with the larger, bulkier items and work my way down to the smaller things.

FLOOR SPACE—When designing your plan, you want to use all of the floor space to your best advantage while still maintaining a nice open area to move around within the closet. If the floor space is all clogged, it makes it very difficult, if not impossible, to get to all of the items in your closet. Ensure that there is always a clear pathway from the door of the closet to all points of access within the closet. Use additional storage units within the closet such as shelving units, cube storage or shoe racks to build up your storage vertically from the floor. The cube unit provides a lot of easily accessible storage for commonly used items while the shoe rack in the back of our closet, which is slightly harder to access, holds footwear that is less frequently used.

WALL SPACE—Wall space is often forgotten when it comes to storage, but can provide a huge amount of easily accessible storage space. All of the wall space in this closet, no matter how small, serves some function. Simple hooks added to the side of the closet hold all of our keys that are not on our daily key chains, while coat hooks in the back of the closet provide easy storage for guests coats, purses and frequently used accessories.

SHELVING—If you still have extra storage needs you can look at including additional shelving in your closet space. Choose the least amount of depth needed to meet your needs. In this closet, our coat hooks doubled as a small shelving unit to hold a basket with the family's sunglasses as well as small flashlight to be able to see into the darker areas of the closet if needed.

Step 4: Reevaluate and Add Additional Organization Products as Needed

It's important to reevaluate any space that you've organized after you've had some time to use it to see if there are any aspects that need to be altered or improved. For this closet, I found that it was a pain trying to access all of the smaller cleaning supplies and accessories that I had stored in one of the cube containers as it was completely jammed full. While there wasn't much room left, I did have some space on the hanging bar and looked around for an idea that might work. A narrow hanging shoe storage unit ended up being the perfect solution and created easily accessible, individual pockets for all of my smaller cleaning items. Taking some time to trial the space before I purchased additional storage let me tailor the organization product to my specific needs.

Organize the Drop Zone

A drop zone is a small area in the entryway (or other convenient space that is close by) to hold all of those little items that you use on a regular basis. It can just be something simple like a shelf, small table or tray for your keys, wallet and other small items, or you could make it a little more elaborate to hold additional items that you think will help improve your organization plan.

Step 1: Decide What Items You Would Like to Include

The easiest way to decide what you want to include in your drop zone is to think about what little items you are commonly looking for when you are running out of the house. This can include sunglasses, wallets, keys, loose change, gum packs or umbrellas. Be sure to have a clear idea of what belongs and doesn't belong in this area. It's not a spot for random clutter, garbage or items that should really be put away elsewhere (such as your paperwork!).

Step 2: Choose a Location

Depending on how much stuff you would like to store, you may wish to have one spot for your items and one spot for your spouse's to keep things separate. Or maybe you will have one spot for the adults and one spot for the kids. Any option is fine—just make sure that it's convenient and that the items are easily accessible to grab on the run.

Step 3: Choose Your Storage Solutions

Now that you have decided what you are going to store and where you want to store it, check to see what space you can use that is already there. Maybe you could add a tray or decorative bin to a shelf or surface top that is already there or put a bin in your bench storage for your drop zone. If all of the areas are already being used, think of alternative storage that you could add such as a small table in the corner, a shelf or wall-mounted basket or storage unit.

Step 4: Finishing Touches

Add your items to the drop zone and make sure that everything has a designated spot. If you have the space, you can always add an item or two to pretty it up a bit such as a little plant or small vase, or add a mirror for a last minute visual inspection as you head out the door.

Organize Seasonal Storage

The last thing that you need to do to create a strong foundation for your entryways is to come up with a plan for all of your seasonal storage. Unless you have a lot of storage space in your entryways or are just really good at keeping only the bare essentials, you will likely need to store at least some of your out-of-season items elsewhere. The following tips can also be applied to storing out-of-season clothing and clothing accessories that you keep in your bedroom closets or when storing clothing items that you plan to use as hand-me-downs in the future.

Step 1: Pick a Location

First you need to decide where you want to store everything when it isn't in season. This could be in your basement, a closet space that is specifically for seasonal items, or in an attic—just be sure that the space is clean, dry and well ventilated. If you are storing out-of-season items in your closet, place them toward the back or high up on the shelves so that the in-season articles can be placed in locations that are more easily accessible. Look for bins that slide underneath your bed for extra storage space (see the DIY Under the Bed Storage Tray on page 126) or use bins that can be stacked up in a taller, narrower space. Unused luggage can also be used for some space-saving storage. Keep all items together in one area, rather than spread out in different locations throughout the house, so they will be easy to find.

Step 2: Sort Through Clothing

There is no point storing clothing items that you no longer wear, so go through all of your items before deciding what you actually need to store. If you didn't wear an item during the current season, it's more than likely that you won't wear it next year either. For items that you did wear, check to make sure that they are still in good condition and that you still like them.

Step 3: Wash Items

Ensure that all clothes are free of stains before storing them. Stains can become set in and very difficult to remove if left through the off-season and can also attract insects. Do not use any starch on shirts as this can also attract bugs. Make sure that everything has thoroughly dried before sealing it away in storage containers to prevent any mold or mildew.

Step 4: Decide How You Want to Store Your Items

Once you have decided on the location, you need to choose how you would like to store your items. Cardboard boxes should NOT be used as they are acidic and the glue that they contain can attract insects. Items should also not be stored in plastic dry cleaning bags as these can trap moisture and encourage mildew. The following methods are best for storing and protecting your clothes from pests and moisture.

VACUUM STORAGE BAGS—If you are short on space, vacuum storage bags can often triple or quadruple your storage space by vacuuming out all of the air and compressing your clothing. These come in a variety of sizes as well as hanging bags.

PLASTIC TOTES—Plastic containers with lids are ideal for storing clothing and you can choose clear containers so you can see exactly what's in there. Clean them with a disinfectant cleaner (or water and vinegar mixture) and then line them with acid-free tissue paper or a cotton sheet to help protect your items prior to storing them.

ZIPPERED CANVAS TOTES OR FABRIC STORAGE BAGS—If you're going to be using fabric storage bags run them through the wash to remove any dust or mold spores. Ensure that they are dried thoroughly before storing to prevent mold and mildew.

Step 5: Protect Your Items

To keep your clothes protected and smelling fresh, add one of these to your storage container:

LAVENDER SACHET—Lavender helps to repel moths, smells lovely and is both antibacterial and antifungal.

CEDAR CHIP SACHET—Cedar naturally repels moths and carpet beetles and also helps to absorb odors.

CHALK—Wrap some pieces of chalk together to help absorb excess moisture from the air.

Step 6: Label Your Containers

Make sure to label your containers so that you know what is inside and can easily find all of your items when they are back in season again.

Tips to Maintain a Healthy Weight in your Entryways and Mudroom

- Do a quick coat check every couple of weeks to ensure that everything is still in its proper place and that extra coats and hoodies have not migrated there from other areas of the house.

- Reevaluate your needs each season as you move items to more long-term storage for the off-season. Donate the item if you didn't use it during its current season—there is no point in storing something you don't use for another year!

- Do a quick check of the drop zone every week to make sure that everything is in its place and that there are no miscellaneous items there that belong elsewhere. This should only take a couple of minutes.

- Ensure that all paperwork goes directly to your paper storage system and does not clog up your entryways.

- Make each family member responsible for putting away their jackets, shoes and any items that they have brought in from outside as soon as they get home. It really requires minimal time but will make your entryways appear so much lighter!

CHAPTER 14

DEFLATING THE GARAGE

The carport or garage is a common area to put all of those items that you don't really know what to do with. Sports equipment, seasonal items, garden supplies and other random clutter can quickly fill up the space and decrease its function. With some basic organization strategies, you can reclaim your garage and create a space that is just as organized and functional as the other rooms in your home.

The warmer, drier months of the year tend to be the best time to declutter the garage, as it is much easier to do if you can pull everything out onto the driveway instead of worrying about keeping everything under cover. If this isn't possible, you may need to work in smaller sections or move some items into the house while you're organizing.

Shedding the Pounds

The garage is often the worst area in the home for packing on the pounds. It's an easy dumping ground for all of that stuff that you don't quite know what to do with, and once the weight starts to accumulate, it just seems to attract more. While I typically like to declutter my rooms one section at a time, I do find that the garage is easier to declutter in one big session. Since it tends to be more of a household catchall, one of the biggest decluttering challenges is determining what should actually stay in the garage and what should go elsewhere. This is much easier to do if you can truly see everything that's in there.

If you don't think that you're up to the task of doing the whole garage at once, you can choose to break it down into the smaller zones (see the next page). Remember that anything is better than nothing, so if you are feeling overwhelmed, just get started on a smaller area and get rid of the weight little by little. Keep the following items in mind as you are sorting through your space to help you drop those pounds.

SPORTS EQUIPMENT—Check out all sporting gear. Toss or recycle items that are in poor condition and donate items that are in good condition that just don't fit you or that you don't use. You may want to consider selling more expensive equipment that's still in really good shape as these often sell well with a good rate of return.

OUTSIDE TOYS—Outside toys can often take quite a beating, so check to make sure that everything you're keeping is still in good working order with all needed parts. Toss or recycle broken items and check that any blow-up items are still holding air. Toys that your kids have outgrown that are still in good condition should be donated or sold.

YARD AND GARDEN EQUIPMENT—Ensure that all equipment is in good working order and that you still use all of the equipment that you are holding on to. When possible, choose equipment that serves multiple purposes rather than a single use. Toss or donate any gadgets that you don't truly need. Keep all accessories to your equipment stored together and label items such as electrical cords and chargers if needed.

YARD AND GARDEN SUPPLIES—Check fertilizers, sprays or other garden supplies that you may have for expired items or items that you don't use. Make sure all hoses and nozzles are in good working order with no cracks.

TOOLS—If you store your tools in the garage, sort through these items and keep only what you actually use. Donate items that you have multiples of and toss items that are in poor condition. If you have more expensive tools or power equipment that you no longer use, these can usually be sold quite easily.

STORAGE BOXES—Look through all storage boxes to ensure that these are filled with items that you still need and use. Do not just pile these back on the shelf. These should all be items that are used at least once per year—not just random items that you don't know what to do with. If these boxes have been sitting in your garage for years and you have barely opened them, be honest with yourself about what you can get rid of. Refer back to Overcoming Your Decluttering Obstacles in Chapter 2 (page 16) if you are having trouble letting go of these items. Make sure that all of the boxes that you are keeping are labeled clearly so you know exactly what is in them. You may even want to put a more detailed inventory list on the inside of the box to make it easier to find what you are looking for.

CAR CARE ITEMS—Assess all of your car care items such as wiper fluid, oil or car wash sprays and keep only those items that you use. If you have car wash items and car waxes that you never use, get rid of them.

OTHER ITEMS—Return all items that you would like to keep but don't belong in the garage to wherever they belong. Put them away immediately when you are finished decluttering the garage.

Building Muscle: The Garage Exercise Plan

The number one rule for the garage is that it should not be a dumping ground for items that you do not have a place for. Think of the garage just like any other room in your home and decide what functions you would like it to have. Since the garage tends to serve many different purposes, start by deciding what functional zones you would like to create. This space can really be anything that you want it to be, so don't just limit it to the traditional functions of holding your car and yard equipment.

The following list gives you an idea of some common garage zones. You likely won't have room (or a need) for all of them in your space—just choose what's most important to you and what will help to improve the function of your home.

VEHICLE ZONE—For most people the number one function of the carport or garage is to create a nice, clear space to park their vehicle. This zone can also include a dedicated space to store any supplies related to automobile care, such as windshield wiper fluid, oil or car cleaning and waxing supplies. If you are happy parking your car out in your driveway, you may decide that you would rather have this large space for another purpose or perhaps will choose to just park your vehicle in the garage during the winter months only.

SPORTS EQUIPMENT ZONE—If you like to live an active lifestyle, the garage often serves as the best place to store all of your sports gear. This area holds any sports equipment or outdoor games, including bikes, scooters, balls, golf equipment, hockey gear, etc.

STORAGE ZONE—The garage can often be used for a variety of storage purposes such as seasonal items, camping items or other bulk items that don't fit easily in your home. If you do use the garage for this purpose, ensure that the items that you are storing are all items that are used at some point throughout the year and are not just items that you don't know what to do with.

WASTE AND RECYCLING ZONE—This zone includes any garbage bins, recycling containers or yard waste bags. Place this area close to the door to your home so that it's easy to access.

TOOL ZONE—If you don't have a basement, the garage is usually the next most common area to store hand tools, power tools and hardware items that are needed for home improvement or other building projects. For some, it may even serve as a workshop.

YARD AND GARDEN EQUIPMENT ZONE—Whether you are an avid gardener or just need to take care of the basic yard care around your home, you will still likely have a variety of yard and equipment items to store. This zone holds your lawnmower, yard and garden power tools such as a blower or trimmer, and smaller garden tools such as a spade and garden gloves. Garden supplies could be stored here as well or kept in the storage zone if it fits your space better. If you have a larger property, you may have a shed or other storage area elsewhere in your yard and don't require a space for this in your garage.

FOOD ZONE—Some people choose to keep a deep freeze or extra refrigerator in their garage and may also store some extra bulk food items as well depending on how stable the temperatures are throughout the year.

MUDROOM AREA—If you are short on entry space in your home and have an attached garage, you can set up a small mudroom area for coat, shoes, and outdoor accessory storage by the garage door leading into your home. See page 167 for more ideas on organizing this space.

Remember that the basic idea of dividing your garage into zones is to group all similar items together and closest to the area that you will be using them in. This gives you quick access to your items as you need them and makes it much easier for everyone to know where to put them away. Once you have decided where the various zones will be located, you can then start planning out how you want to organize your items and what storage solutions you may need.

Because the garage can serve so many functions, it's even more important that you build a strong foundation to hold all of the weight that your garage will be carrying.

General Garage Organization

Now that you have an idea of the various garage zones, it's time to get going on your plan. I will talk in greater detail about organizing strategies and ideas for some of these zones later in the chapter, but the basic principles will be the same for all of them and ideas from one space can always be applied to another. Follow the steps outlined below to design and implement a functional and organized garage space for you and your family.

Step 1: Choose the Functional Zones

Based on the needs of your family and the space that you have available, choose what zones you want to create in your garage. Start with those areas that are your top priorities and see what space you have left for other less important zones when these are completed.

Step 2: Empty the Garage

If you have a full day or weekend to devote to cleaning out your garage, I would highly recommend clearing everything out at once. I really find that this a much easier way to get things done and a much better way to visualize how you would like to see things put back in. If this is not possible, however, or if you find it too overwhelming to deal with everything at once, you can start to work on it by individual zones starting at one end of the garage and working towards the other end as you progress.

As you empty out the items, sort them into your keep, toss, donate and belongs elsewhere piles. Keep your zones in mind to determine if the items that you are keeping should be in the keep or belongs elsewhere pile and keep your similar items together as much as possible.

Step 3: Clean

Now that your garage space is empty, give it a good cleaning, getting rid of any cobwebs in the corners and dust on the shelves. Sweep and wash the floor or hose or power wash it down if it's particularly dirty and you have a drainage system to handle the water. If the floor is in rough shape, you could consider painting it if you have the time available. Allow the floor to completely dry before putting anything away.

Step 4: Choose Storage Solutions

Before you start loading things back in, take a look around at any current storage solutions that you have previously implemented in your garage. What areas work well and what areas do you need to look at adding additional storage solutions? Keeping your zones in mind, place items that you already have storage for back in their appropriate zones and then evaluate what items and how much space you have left.

SHELVING—If you are handy with tools, it's fairly easy to install basic wooden shelving units in the garage. If you have a lot of storage needs, aim for floor-to-ceiling shelving to optimize your space and store less frequently used and lighter items up higher while keeping more frequently used items within arms' reach. These would be quite inexpensive to have built for you by a handyman or contractor if building them yourself is beyond your skill set. You can also look at metal or plastic shelving options from big-box or organization stores if you have a little more money to spend.

WALL STORAGE UNITS—To get the most out of your garage space, use as much of the wall space for storage as possible, in order to keep the floor clear for other uses. There are many DIY options or prefabricated storage units that work great in the garage for storing a variety of items as well as units that are designed specifically for specific equipment such as storing bikes, holding ladders or keeping ski equipment together.

Pegboard is another inexpensive and functional way to store a variety of items that may be in your garage such as sports equipment, garden tools or home improvement tools. These units can be customized with hooks, shelves and baskets to accommodate a variety of storage needs, and are easy to switch around as your needs change. See the DIY Pegboard Organizer (page 189) for details on how to easily build your own.

CEILING STORAGE—If you are short on space, the ceiling is another great option for storing items, especially those that you don't need regular access to. There are many different metal storage units that are designed to be mounted to the ceiling to hold storage bins, as well as ceiling racks that are specifically designed for bikes or other sports equipment.

Step 5: Reevaluate

Once all of your additional storage has been added, return any remaining items to their dedicated space. Try out your organization system for a couple of weeks and then take a little time to evaluate how everything is working. The garage, in particular, may take a little tweaking here and there after it's organized to make sure that it's functioning as effectively as possible. If certain areas are difficult to access or tend to be accumulating a little extra clutter already, see if any other storage options may be possible. Remember that the simpler something is to do, the more likely it will be done.

Organize the Yard Equipment

Even small yards require some basic yard and garden equipment and the requirements can quickly grow with the size of your yard. To make things even more difficult, these tools are often large and bulky, making them more difficult to store. Once you have pared down your equipment to your minimal needs, you'll need to find a dedicated spot for each item.

To help keep the floor clean in this area, consider putting some rubber mats down over the floor. These can easily be taken out if covered in dirt or yard clippings and hosed down. To best organize your supplies, divide them into smaller categories based on their purpose such as yard power tools, smaller garden tools and basic supplies. Once you have all of your categories identified and know how much space you need for each of them, you can start thinking of the best storage solutions.

GARDEN TOOLS—Wall-mounted storage pegs or hooks work well for hanging long-handled tools or lighter-weight power tools and free up some much needed floor space. If this isn't an option, you can look at floor units that have specific slots to hold your tools upright. Smaller garden tools work well hung from a pegboard (see page 189 for instructions) or other wall hooks or could be stored in a plastic bin or other container.

SUPPLIES—Bagged garden supplies such as soil or fertilizer are best stored in a plastic tub or other container in case of any spills. If you do keep them out, ensure that the bags are all sealed properly and there aren't any sharp tools around that could poke into them. If you are short on garage space, you could also store these supplies outside in a clean garbage bin.

POWER TOOLS—Larger yard power tools need to be stored properly to keep them in good working order and away from young children. Keep them grouped in one location, usually around where you store your lawn mower. Keep any fuel stored away safely and be sure to empty the fluids from the units when storing them over the off-season. To save space with your lawn mower look for more compact units or a model with a folding handle.

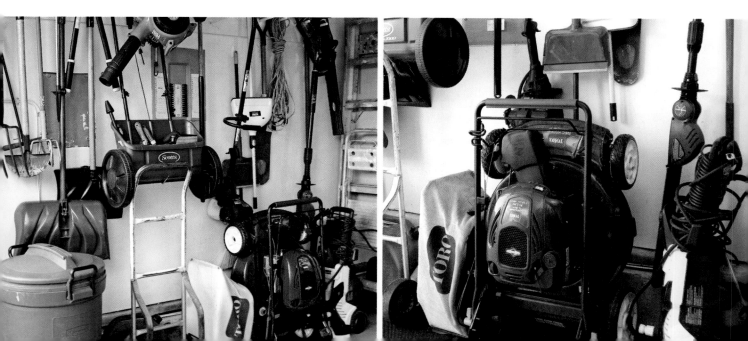

Organize the Sports Equipment

If you have a sports-loving family, you likely have a variety of sports equipment around your home that's in need of some organization. Sports equipment can be difficult to organize due to all of the different shapes and sizes, especially if you participate in multiple sports. When dividing your equipment up, you can either organize it by sport or organize it more by type (such as all of the balls and pucks together, all of the protective gear stored together, etc.). There are many different equipment organizers available on the market for sport-specific gear as well as multisport organizers.

Whatever storage method you choose, you want to find storage solutions that protect your gear while taking up the least amount of space. If the equipment is for your children, you ideally want them to be able to grab (and put away!) the equipment themselves. Look to floor units to hold sticks, bats, skis or other tall, thin equipment or create your own storage from an old pallet.

Shoe racks or other shelving units can be used to hold sport-specific footwear as well as bins or baskets containing smaller equipment such as small balls or protective pads. A clean garbage bin could hold larger balls or other gear that is awkward to store. Use wall storage as much as possible for items that can be hung to free up floor space as much as possible.

DIY Pegboard Organizer

Pegboards are fabulous for organizing all of those little items that you are not quite sure what to do with and allow you to easily find whatever you are looking for. Even though this one is used for our sports storage, pegboards also work great for organizing craft supplies, tools, kitchen gadgets, cleaning supplies and more. They can be used in pretty much any space or room in your home, are inexpensive to buy, can easily be cut down to any size and are an easy project to install. We used twelve 2 x 2 foot (60 x 60 cm) pieces that we cut down from 4 x 8 foot (122 x 243 cm) boards, but you can really choose whatever size you would like. If you are not comfortable cutting them down, most home-supply stores will cut them for you—just have your measurements ready! While it was easier to paint them this way since I was doing a checkerboard pattern (I spray-painted mine with a paint sprayer), they would be a little easier to mount to your frame if you leave them in the larger sheets. The pegboard needs to be mounted onto a frame because the hooks need clearance space behind the pegboard.

Pegboard

Pine 1 x 2 boards for the frame

Miter saw

3-inch (7.5 cm) wood screws

Stud finder

Plastic anchors (if you are unable to mount to studs)

³/₄-inch (2-cm) wood screws and washers

Screw gun or drill

Hooks and holders

Step 1: Cut and Paint the Pegboard
Cut the pegboard and 1 x 2 frames to the desired sizes.

Step 2: Build the Pegboard Frame
Lay out all of the pieces out on the floor to make sure that the measurements are correct and then screw them together using the ³/₄-inch (2-cm) wood screws. Note: We raised ours up off the floor on 2 x 4s to make it easier to use the drill.

Step 3: Mount the Frame to the Wall
Mark where the studs are on the wall and mount the frame to the wall using screws (we used 3-inch [7-cm] screws into the studs). If you are unable to screw into studs, make sure to use plastic anchors for the drywall. Use a framing square and/or a level to ensure that the frame is level and square at the corners.

Step 4: Mount the Pegboard onto the Frame
Using ³/₄-inch (19-mm) screws and a drill, mount the pegboard onto the frame. Starting in one corner, align the outer edges of the pegboard and space the screws evenly. We had to use a jigsaw on one of our pegboard pieces to cut a small square to accommodate a light switch.

Step 5: Add the Finishing Touches
Add hooks, holders and bins to hold your gear. This can easily be switched up at any time as your needs change. Make sure your kids are able to reach and put away their own items as much as possible.

Organize the Waste/Recycling

If you store your garbage and recycling bins in your garage, it's important to keep this area well organized and free of clutter. Maintaining the cleanliness of the space makes collection day easier.

When choosing the location of your garbage zone, keep it as close as possible to the door to your home so you can easily drop in garbage and recycling as it accumulates. Since little spills are inevitable in this area, you may wish to put down a rubber mat under your bins to help contain any mess. These can then be taken outside for a hose down when needed. You also want to make sure that the containers you have for your garbage and recycling are large enough to hold the waste that you produce each week. Constant overflow can be difficult and time consuming to clean up. Keep garbage and recycling bags close by.

With all of the waste that's produced these days, it's important to recycle whenever we can. Check your local municipal guidelines to see what items are recyclable and what items need to be brought to a specific recycling facility, such as paint cans or electronics, as well as how they require the recycling to be sorted and put out for collection. Keep all items needed for this in one location.

Step 1: Empty and Clean Out the Space

In order to give this space a good cleaning, you need to have everything out. Spray down the area with a disinfectant spray if possible and give it a thorough scrubbing. Also hose down and disinfect any bins that you have previously used. Allow everything to completely dry and bring your bins out into the sun if possible for some added natural disinfecting.

Step 2: Choose the Containers

If your bins are not provided, choose your containers based on the space that you have available and the amount of storage that you need to contain everything. You could just use garbage bins for this or look for more stackable options to cut down on the space required. Either way, make sure that all bins are easily accessible. Front access allows bins to be stacked and light weight makes for easy portability and cleaning purposes.

Step 3: Label the Containers

Label everything clearly so that everyone in your family knows where each item goes. By separating the recycling into the appropriate categories as you go, you save a lot of time and avoid messing around with dirty containers when it comes to putting it out for collection. Choose labels that can get wet and can easily be wiped down so that you don't have to worry about them when you're cleaning your containers. I used a chalk pen on mine (Artista Pro® Chalk Ink) that requires an ammonia-based cleaner so it doesn't smudge when wiped down with water.

Step 4: Determine Your Maintenance Plan

This area tends to get a little dirtier than others, so come up with a regular maintenance plan to keep the area clean. Bins should be washed down at least every couple of weeks after you have completely emptied them for collection. Check yearly for any updates that your area may have on recycling capabilities and restrictions, as these can change. If you find that you have more recycling than you can handle, look for other ways to cut down on your waste such as not using bottled water or buying more bulk items with less packaging.

Organizing the Storage

While it's fine to have a storage area in your garage, you want this to be for useful items—not just random junk or leftover boxes that you never bothered to unpack when you moved. Take some time to look at what you actually have stored in your garage and what items you really need to keep. Return items that you may have borrowed or those objects that belong elsewhere in your home. This section helps you to define what items should and shouldn't be stored in your garage.

Step 1: Sort Through Storage Items

Bring all storage boxes and random items that have just been tossed in the garage to one location. If you have the space and the time, you can go through everything at once. Otherwise you may just want to sort through one or two boxes per day to make it less overwhelming. Ideally you want to empty everything out of the boxes; however, if you are sure that you know all of the contents in the box and that you need everything in there, you may be able to skip this step for some boxes. Sort your items into the keep, donate, toss and belongs elsewhere piles. If you haven't even looked in the boxes for years, chances are they just need to go!

Step 2: Sort the Keep Pile

Go through all of the keep items and sort into similar categories or by season needed. Be sure that you really need and will use all of these items. If you haven't used them in the last year, they should probably be added to your donate pile.

Step 3: Condense the Bins

How you pack your items into the bins can really make a big difference in how much space they take up. For bins that you only need access to once or twice per year such as those containing seasonal decorations or summer gear, package everything up as space efficiently as possible. If you have containers, store smaller items inside of them to fill up the empty space as much as possible. Nest items and fill in any gaps in the container with smaller items when possible. Ensure that all breakables are stored safely and wrapped in tissue or a small amount of bubble wrap. If it's difficult to see all of the items in the bin, write out an inventory list to place on top of the bin so you will know exactly what's in there.

For those bins that you need access to on a more regular basis, you may sacrifice some of the space-saving strategies to allow for easier access and visibility. Keep these bins less full so you can really see what's in there and have some space to move things around to grab what you need.

Step 4: Label and Store

Make sure that all bins are clearly labeled on the outside of the bin. If you have an item that does not fit any of your garage storage categories, it either does not belong in the garage or you need to ensure that you have the space and a specific location to actually store it. Do not let random items that have nowhere to go pile up!

Store bins that you need access to more regularly at chest level or below so you can easily access them. Bins that are only needed once or twice per year can be stored higher up on shelving units or with ceiling-storage options. Avoid stacking bins one on top of each other whenever possible and stick to the one-step storage rule: every bin should be accessible with one step rather than having to move a couple of other boxes or bins out of the way first. This keeps things simple and makes it easier for you to keep things neat and tidy.

Tips to Maintain a Healthy Weight in the Garage

Since the garage tends to be one of the areas of your home that puts on weight the easiest, taking time to develop some good organization habits in this area can go a long way in maintaining your healthy space.

- Rinse out recycling bins every couple of weeks immediately after the recycling goes out. Add additional bins if needed if you find that they are constantly overflowing.

- Review seasonal storage bins at the end of each season. Donate or toss any items that weren't used. Sort through holiday items at the start of the season as charities will often not take these once the season is over.

- Reevaluate yard and garden supplies and equipment at the start and end of gardening season. Toss or donate any items that you did not use throughout the season and ensure that all items are cleaned and in proper working order before storing them away at the end of the season.

- Do a thorough cleaning of the garage space at least twice per year. Remove as many items as possible (or at least the items on the floor) and give it a good sweep or hose down.

- Wipe down outdoor tools after each use so you are not bringing excessive amounts of dirt or grass into the garage space.

- Empty fluids from seasonal equipment when you are storing it in the off-season.

CHAPTER 15

CURTAILING THE BONUS ROOMS

You have made it to the last stages of the plan, and now it's time to work on any extra bonus rooms that are more unique to your own home. This could be your basement, craft room, games room, attic space or whatever other rooms and spaces you have not yet tackled. By now you've hopefully learned all of the steps needed to tackle any space in your home on your own, so it's time to put it all into practice!

Shedding the Pounds

Use everything that you have learned in the previous chapters to come up with your own list of items that you need to let go. These are items that don't serve a purpose in your home, items that you don't use or love, or items that don't represent who you actually are today. Refer back to Chapter 2 on page 13 if you ever need ideas or motivation to help you on your decluttering mission.

Building Strength: Exercises for the Bonus Rooms

No matter what room you're organizing, think about building a strong organization system to support all of the weight. While it may take more intentional planning at first, the more areas you organize, the easier this process will become. Here are the basic steps that you want to go through with any space.

Step 1: Identify the Zones
Identify the functions that you need the space to provide. Think of the room in zones.

Step 2: Remove and Sort the Items
Sort all of the items that you're keeping into similar categories so you roughly know how much space you'll need and how you would like to organize your items. Get rid of a little extra weight if possible and purge a few more items.

Step 3: Choose Storage Options
Based on the space available and what you need to store, choose smart storage solutions that can be used in your space. Keep things as simple as possible to make it easier to maintain.

Step 4: Return Items Based on Zone Plan
Put all of the items back into the space and add any decorative touches to make the space your own.

Step 5: Reevaluate Plan
After you have had a chance to try out the system, take some time to evaluate how everything is working. Make any adjustments as needed.

Tips to Maintain a Healthy Weight in Bonus Rooms

The last part of the process is to think about simple ways to help maintain your organized space. What areas do you think you will have to monitor more closely? What weekly, monthly or quarterly check-ins could you do to ensure that everything is staying the way you like?

CHAPTER 16

DEVELOPING HEALTHY HABITS: MAINTAINING YOUR HEALTHY HOME LIFESTYLE

Creating and, most importantly, maintaining an organized home is really about developing some simple, healthy lifestyle habits and integrating them into your regular daily routines—just as maintaining a healthy lifestyle of diet and exercise would be after going on a diet. The Home Decluttering Diet is designed to be followed on an ongoing basis and repeated each year for general maintenance. After you have completed the first year, each subsequent year's tune-ups should be quicker and easier to accomplish with just minor adjustments as your family needs change. This chapter focuses on how to keep the clutter out and some basic organization habits to adopt. They may not all be for you, so try them out and see what works best for your specific family and lifestyle.

A truly organized space should really be quite easy to maintain with just a few minor habit changes, so if your space is starting to get cluttered again quickly, take some time to evaluate what the problems are. Is there just too much stuff in the space? Are items difficult to access and require a lot of shuffling around to get to them? Are things getting put back in the wrong spot? Sometimes you just need to be a little more diligent about putting things away once you use them, but other times require a bit more reworking. Once you have figured out what the problems are, you can do a little tweaking to get things back on track: maybe you need to do a little more decluttering, purchase a bin or two to corral similar items together or label the designated storage areas so everyone knows where things go. Recognize when the pounds are starting to creep back on and address them immediately.

As you go through each room every year, you have a chance to evaluate what is working and what isn't. This allows you to keep on top of things and address problem areas before they get too far out of hand. Some rooms or specific spots in rooms tend to gain weight more than others, so you may need to spend a little extra time in specific areas maybe you still need to declutter and shed a few more pounds or perhaps a few new organization solutions will build the muscle you need to keep things organized. Whatever you do, don't give up on the plan—sometimes just a little change or two will make a big difference!

Tips for Keeping the Clutter Out

Now that you have a more decluttered home, the trick is obviously to keep it that way! Likely there were some bad habits that got you into your mess in the first place, so unless these are addressed, that clutter has a good chance of returning. The following healthy habits will help you maintain your home's current weight, so practice these on a regular basis and integrate them into your new lifestyle.

Everything Has a Place and Everything in its Place

If you have followed The Home Decluttering Diet, you should have already created a specific spot for all of the items in your home, so get in the habit of putting things back where they belong as soon as you are finished with them. Before you let new items come into your home, ensure that you have a place that they can go and that all of your family members know where that place is as well. If you are finding that certain items are consistently not being put back where they belong, ask yourself why this is happening. Is the storage area not accessible enough? Maybe you need to modify your organization system a bit. Do your family members not know where it goes? Make sure containers or baskets are clearly labeled. Or is it just simply a matter of being lazy about putting it away?

Don't Get Sucked in by Sales

If you are one of those people who just can't pass up a good deal, think very carefully before you make that purchase! Remember that every item that you bring into your home has a price, a price of time to clean and maintain it, a price of space and a price of energy. No matter how good the deal is (even if it is free!), if you don't need it or and will not use it, leave it for someone else who will. You don't need that extra weight! Be especially wary of those "Buy 2 Get 1 Free" deals or stores that will sell at a slightly discounted price if you buy multiple items. If you do not need it, do not buy it! If you do end up with a free item that you don't need, give it to a friend who needs it or place it immediately in the donate bin.

Do Not Buy Things That You Can't Return

This one might not apply to everyone and, of course, there are always a few exceptions, but for me, I need to see things in my house before I know if they are going to work. I probably end up taking back at least a quarter of everything that I buy because it either doesn't work in the space like I had envisioned or I decide that I really don't need it. Clothing that looked fabulous in the store doesn't look quite as good when I get it home or doesn't really go with anything else in my closet. Home decor items don't fit on the shelf that I had originally purchased it for. Remember that you truly want to love everything that you keep! That great deal on a clearance item that you can't return may not end up being such a great deal after all if you never end up using it.

Do Not Buy Things for Your Future Self

Have you ever bought something because you believed that you would need it in the future or you wished you had enough time to be able to use it? I used to be bad about doing this, and at least half of the time I never ended up using the item. Buy items as you need them instead of predicting what you will be doing/wanting/needing at some future time. Sure a small little stockpile of food or basic items like toilet paper or paper towels is fine every now and then, but don't go overboard here. While you may believe that you are going to need that yoga mat next year when your child is finally off to kindergarten, it might not happen! Live in the present and leave the future clear for whatever it may hold.

Keep at Least 20 Percent Free Space in Storage Areas

First you need to recognize that your home has a finite amount of space. You can only pack your cupboards so full or stuff so much into your closets. If a space is filled to its maximum capacity, it can be more difficult to keep it organized and see everything that is in there. Over time, items don't get put back in the right spot, things get messy and you can't find what you are looking for. Always keep at least a little space open to give yourself a little freedom of movement to shuffle items around or to accommodate other items that you may need to add.

Follow the "Calories In, Calories Out" Rule

Again this doesn't always work out, but basically when you get something new, ask yourself if it is replacing something that you now no longer need or will no longer use. Think back again to how calories work with weight loss: to maintain weight, the calories consumed needs to equal the calories burned. I find that this works especially well with clothing items, kids' toys and other small household items. For example, if you buy a new pair of boots, are they replacing a worn-out pair that you can no longer wear (that you can now toss out) or did you just not have any boots to start with? On the other hand, if you already have three pairs of beautiful boots that you don't want to get rid of in exchange for the new ones, maybe you don't really need those new boots after all!

Reevaluate and Modify

Life is constantly changing and the needs of your family will constantly be changing with it. The items that you require when you have young children in the house are different than if you have teenagers and become quite different again when you become an empty nester or have never had children. Just as our caloric needs change over time, so does the amount of stuff that we require in our homes.

Have a Permanent Donation Box

I keep one large donation box in the garage as well as a few smaller boxes in each of our bedroom closets so that I can put items in immediately when I determine that I no longer need or want them. This helps to keep me from second-guessing if I should really be getting rid of it and keeps the space from getting overwhelmed with items that I am no longer using. Once the box starts to get full, I make a quick trip to drop it off. Doing small amounts of decluttering as you go is so much simpler!

Tips for Keeping Things Tidy and Organized on a Daily Basis

Focusing on a few small daily habits can actually have a huge impact on the overall tidiness and organization of your home, and once you have been working on them for a while, you won't even think twice before doing them.

Start By Making the Bed

I know some people think that making the bed is a waste of time, but it really makes a big difference in how tidy the room looks and only takes a couple of minutes to do. Plus, I think that it starts off the day well and I love climbing into a made bed at the end of the day. To make things easier, simplify your bedding as much as possible. Cut out your top sheet and just use a duvet with a washable cover, minimize the number of pillows on your bed or use a large enough comforter that you don't need to perfectly tuck in your sheets.

Never Leave a Room Empty Handed

This is one habit that can make a huge difference in the general tidiness of your home. As you move from one room to another (or from one floor to another), do a quick scan to see if there is anything that you can take with you that belongs where you are going. Take only what you will have time to put away—moving a pile from one room to another without actually putting anything away doesn't really help you out much. It can be a couple of dirty dishes that you put in the dishwasher or some laundry that needs to be put away upstairs. Always keep in mind the "One Touch" rule, meaning that you ideally only want to touch items one time before they are put away. Every time you touch an object to move it from one place to another you are using up precious time and energy so make that extra little effort to put it directly away. Again, I think it is really more about habit than not having the time.

Get the Whole Family Involved

This one might take a while to accomplish, but it's definitely one of the habits that will make the biggest positive impact in the overall organization and function of your home. Yes, it's often actually easier to just put things away yourself, but spending the time to teach your children to do age-appropriate tasks will be better in the long run for both of you. Start by just working on having your kids pick up after themselves—putting their coat and shoes away when they come in the house, cleaning their toys up each night, etc. It's amazing how much of a difference it can make in the overall tidiness of the house if just these simple things are done. Include them in the decision making when you are working on decluttering and organizing their spaces, and ensure that all of their belongings are kid-accessible. For the first few weeks that you do this, you will likely need to monitor your kids a lot, but over time this will start to be a habit for them as well and it should eventually be able to be done with minimal reminders.

Do a 15-Minute Nightly Clean-Up

Make it a routine to do a family 15-minute nightly tidy-up. For some reason it doesn't seem quite so bad to tidy up when everyone else is doing the same thing. Put on the timer and just stick with the top cleaning priorities. Kids can clean their rooms or do other small household chores while you finish up the kitchen cleaning or fold and put away laundry. Start with the things that are making the biggest mess or creating a lot of clutter or any "must dos" that need to be done before bed.

Recognize Your Home's Hot Spots

We all have those places in our homes where the clutter tends to accumulate and we put weight on the most easily. Oftentimes, it's the front entrance or kitchen counter, but it can really be anywhere. These are often good areas to check regularly for quick tune-ups. Figure out what items end up there and create a new home for them. If it's not needed, get rid of it!

Closing Thoughts

Achieving your happy and healthy home may not always be easy, but it's definitely attainable and well worth the journey. I hope that The Home Decluttering Diet has helped you to look at decluttering and organizing in a new way and given you the inspiration to achieve your goals—or at least take the big leap to get started on the process. The road to an organized home never really ends, but the path will get easier as you continue to build on the strong organization systems that you've started. Keep this book close and continue to follow the monthly maintenance plan to avoid any weight gain and reinforce all of the healthy organization habits that you've learned. Think often about all that you've achieved and enjoy the more peaceful home that you've created.

ACKNOWLEDGMENTS

First, I would like to thank my family, without whom I would not have been able to write this book. This process has definitely been a labor of love, and I could not have done it without your love and support. To my husband, who picked up the slack around the house and made sure that we were all fed when I could not get off the computer. To my parents, who entertained my children so I could get in some uninterrupted work time and to my Dad, who spent many hours helping me bring all of my projects to life. Finally, to my boys, Matthew and Connor, who are truly the inspiration behind it all.

I would also like to thank all of my amazing blog readers who have continued to inspire me throughout this organization journey. I am so thankful for your emails, comments and support and hope that this book offers you some inspiration in return.

Thank you to my workplace, The Fraser Valley Child Development Center, for allowing me to take some much needed time off to complete the book and to my hardworking colleagues for covering my caseload in my absence.

Last, I would like to thank Page Street Publishing for giving me the opportunity to bring my dream to reality. Writing a book goes beyond my wildest expectations and I would never have thought it possible without your belief in me.

ABOUT THE AUTHOR

Jennifer Lifford lives in Mission, BC, with her husband and two boys. She is the owner and creator of the lifestyle blog Clean and Scentsible (www.cleanandscentsible.com) where she shares home organization and easy DIY projects, cleaning tips and home decor ideas. Her organization and cleaning tips have been featured in *Better Homes and Gardens* and *HGTV* magazines as well as numerous online publications.

INDEX